CHRIST AND ORIGINAL SIN

CHRIST AND ORIGINAL SIN is one of the IMPACT BOOKS, a series designed to bring the modern reader the significant achievements of scholars, both Catholic and non-Catholic, in the fields of Scripture, Theology, Philosophy, Mathematics, History, and the Physical and Social Sciences. Among the titles in the series are:

The School Examined: An Essay on the Curriculum by Vincent Smith

Catholic Thought in Crisis by Rev. Peter Riga

Introducing the Old Testament by Frederick L. Moriarty, S.J.

This Good News: An Introduction to the Catholic Theology of the New Testament by Quentin Quesnell, S.J.

Maturing in Christ: St. Paul's Program for Growth in Christ by George Montague, S.M.

Seven Books of Wisdom by Roland Murphy, O.Carm.

New Testament Essays by Raymond Brown, S.S.

God and Contemporary Man by Robert J. Kreyche

With the Eyes of Faith by Rev. John L. Murphy

Catechetics by Alfred McBride, O.Praem.

The God of Exodus by James Plastaras, C.M.

The Biblical Meaning of Man by Dom Wulstan Mork, O.S.B.

The Gospel of Eternal Life by Dominic M. Crossan, O.S.M.

The Word Dwells Among Us by William E. Lynch, C.M.

The Person and the Group by John Thornhill, S.M.

Christ and Original Sin

by PETER DE ROSA

THE BRUCE PUBLISHING COMPANY / MILWAUKEE

NIHIL OBSTAT:

John A. Schulien, S.T.D.
Censor librorum

IMPRIMATUR:

✠ William E. Cousins
Archbishop of Milwaukee
March 2, 1967

The Nihil obstat and Imprimatur are a declaration that a book or pamphlet is considered to be free from doctrinal or moral error. It is not implied that those who have granted the Nihil obstat and Imprimatur agree with the contents, opinions, or statements expressed.

Library of Congress Catalog Card Number: 67–19791

TO
MY MOTHER AND FATHER

ACKNOWLEDGMENTS

We are grateful to the following publishers for permission to cite from copyrighted materials:

Harper & Row, Inc., New York, and William Collins & Sons, Ltd., London, for citations from *The Divine Milieu* by Pierre Teilhard de Chardin, © 1960 by Harper & Row, Inc., and William Collins & Sons, Ltd.;

Helicon Press, Inc., Baltimore, and Darton, Longman, and Todd, London, for citations from *Theological Investigations*, Vol. 5 by Karl Rahner, © 1966 by Helicon Press, Inc., and Darton, Longman, and Todd;

B. Herder Book Co., St. Louis, for citations from *The Mysteries of Christianity* by Matthias Scheeben;

Herder & Herder, Inc., New York, for citations from *Jesus Christ* by Yves Congar and from *Theology of Revelation* by Gabriel Moran;

The Paulist Press, New York, and Burns, Oates, London, for citations from *Concilium*, Vol. 11, *Who Was Jesus of Nazareth?*;

Sheed & Ward, Inc., New York, for citations from *Sin, Liberty and Law* by Louis Monden, © 1965 by Sheed & Ward, Inc., from *A Theology of History* by Hans Urs von Balthasar, © 1963 by Sheed & Ward, Inc., and from *A Path Through Genesis* by Bruce Vawter, © 1956 by Sheed & Ward, Inc.;

Templegate Publishers, Springfield, and Geoffrey Chapman, Ltd., London, for citations from *On Trying to Be Human* by Rosemary Haughton.

Contents

CHRIST AND ORIGINAL SIN

PART I

Introduction to the incarnation and original sin

INTRODUCTION

Few subjects are as exciting as theology. This is what we should expect, of course, and yet few of us think of it in fact as an exciting and stimulating science. If we begin to dabble in theology it is hardly with a sense of high adventure. On the contrary, we imagine it to be a rather dull, arduous, abstract, undertaking, perhaps not unlike a research into antiquities for which we have no genuine taste but to which we commit ourselves for a while out of a sense of duty.

Since this notion is so widespread I have undertaken in this book to present two studies in contemporary theology. Here is, so to speak, theology in the making. My wish is that the reader, like myself, should witness the thrilling sight of scholars at work exploring our faith which, although in substance unchanging, continually opens up to the insistent inquirer new avenues for investigation. This is to say that the mind illumined by the Holy

1

Spirit seeks in every generation to understand anew the revelation of God which comes to us in Christ. Without such a search, the faith will not seem pertinent to our lives and times.

The two subjects I have chosen to deal with here are the incarnation and original sin. The selection is determined by my conviction that their treatment by theologians seems to have undergone very recently a marked shift of emphasis. A close analysis of what has happened and is still happening will enable us to follow the discussions of the coming years with a livelier and more enlightened interest. Perhaps I should outline in this introduction the course that our reflections are likely to take.

THE INCARNATION

In the early Church

Many scholars today are convinced that the insistence on Christ's divinity in the presentation of the Catholic faith has tended to obscure the true humanity of Jesus.

It might be said that there has always been the temptation to minimize the reality of Christ's manhood. The first heretics in the early Church were the docetists who claimed that Christ was not truly man but only seemed to be a man. At the end of the second century Clement of Alexandria suggested that because the Word of God was in Christ he had no real need of food as we have, nor did he suffer or rejoice as we do.

> For he ate, not for the sake of the body, which was kept together by a holy energy, but in order that it might not enter into the minds of those who were with him to entertain a different opinion of him. . . . But he was entirely impassible, inaccessible to any movement of feeling, either pleasure or pain.[1]

---

[1] James M. Carmody, S.J., and Thomas E. Clarke, S.J., *Word and Redeemer* (Glen Rock, N. J.: The Paulist Press, 1966), p. 27.

By reason of his curious philosophy of man, Clement thought that there was not in Christ even courage or zeal or joy. "They are inadmissible in the case of the perfect man," he wrote, "who is incapable of exercising courage; for neither does he meet what inspires fear, as he regards none of the things that occur in life as to be dreaded."

In the fourth century Hilary of Poitiers asserted that our Lord "felt the force of suffering but without its pain." The nails pierced his flesh, as an object passes through the air, painlessly.

> Our Lord Jesus Christ suffered blows, hanging, crucifixion and death: but the suffering which attacked the body of the Lord, without ceasing to be suffering, had not the natural effect of suffering. It exercised its function of punishment with all its violence; but the body of Christ by its virtue suffered the violence of the punishment without consciousness of it.[2]

Hilary could not judge of Christ's flesh conceived of the Holy Spirit on the analogy of an ordinary human body. Christ's humanity was from God, hence its freedom from pain, its capacity for transfiguration, its power to walk on water.

In these interesting passages from two great fathers of the Church we see that in their desire to attribute perfection to Christ's manhood they seem to us to make him *less than human.* It is with their very conception of what constitutes perfect manhood that we disagree. But besides their sometimes curious estimate of Christ's humanity, the fathers, from the fourth century onward, had also to contend with the heresy of Arianism. Arius believed Christ to be no more than a man dwelt in by the Word of God and so subordinate to God the Creator. This particular heresy threatened to overwhelm the Church, and it is doubtful whether the Church has yet recovered from the traumatic effect of its onslaught. Since that time, theologians have stepped on each others' heels to tell their fellow Christians that "Jesus is God." Whereas Christ's humanity, it was presumed, was obvious to everyone, his divinity needed to be proclaimed from the house-tops all the while.

---

[2] *Ibid.,* p. 69.

In mediaeval times

Such was the situation in the West in mediaeval times. Anti-Arianism was still the major (albeit unconscious) preoccupation. This meant that the co-equality of Son and Father was to the fore in theological writing and discussion. Furthermore, an even stranger idea of what perfect manhood consisted in held sway among the mediaevals than was to be found in Cyril and Hilary. In the first instance, Adam was credited with amazing privileges of mind and body. A *fortiori*, it was argued, Christ, the second Adam, was deemed to be more perfect still. Not that anyone, to my knowledge, said Jesus was impassible. In fact, from the early middle ages there was a great devotion to the passion and cross of our divine redeemer. Curiously, however, there grew up simultaneously with this devotion a theology of Christ which put him beyond all human efforts at identification and imitation. To him was attributed the beatific vision of his Father from his conception, and an angelic knowledge of the whole of human history. Such things were thought to be entailed by Christ's divinity: if Jesus was God, he must have had a perfect humanity. Perfection was conceived in an excessively platonic fashion, as is evident. Jesus was not tempted as we are; he had no need to struggle as we do.

The rift between theology and devotion which occurred at that time has never been quite healed and sometimes it has grown to dangerous proportions.

Contrasting the old and the new

Perhaps the best way to sketch the christology of contemporary theologians is by contrasting their presentation with that of their immediate predecessors. In books of an earlier period we used to come across sentences like these: "Jesus was God. He proved he was God by his miracles, especially the final miracle of raising himself from the dead."

(i) *"Jesus was God."* This was considered to be the first and central affirmation of theology. When it was said that Jesus must predominate in all our teaching, it was mostly taken to mean that we must stress his divinity beyond, and often in practice apart from, everything else. However, to call Jesus "God" without qualification is already to obscure the trinitarian structure of our faith. Almost without exception when the New Testament uses the word "God" the reference is to the Father who effects our salvation by sending his Son into the world and glorifying him when he had sacrificed himself in love on Calvary. Here I would merely remark that we should be much more aware than we usually are of the influence of language upon thought. I have come across a book for six-year-old children in which the word "God" is used indiscriminately of the Father, the Son, the Holy Spirit and the Trinity — all within about eight lines. No wonder children look upon the Trinity as a puzzle!

By centering exclusively on Jesus as God we do not merely obscure the basic trinitarian structure of our faith — everything coming from God (the Father) and returning to him through Christ and in the power of the Spirit — we tend to answer every theological difficulty with the retort "because Jesus is God." Is it sufficient to pray always or nearly always to Jesus when one considers that most prayers in the New Testament are addressed to the Father? "Of course, because Jesus is God," comes the reply. Why were we redeemed by Christ? Because he died upon the cross for us and he was God. How did Christ represent all of us? Because of his uniqueness: he was not only man but God. As one author puts it:

> Christ is not the product of some evolution of creation and the human race, but a unique "breaking-in" of God upon his creation. . . . He is by nature Head, Chief, King, Master, Teacher of all mankind for ever and ever. . . . He can, therefore, act in the name of all mankind in order to atone for sin and, since the least of his human acts is of infinite value because it is the act

of a divine Person, he will make superabundant reparation for sin, and from him, who is God, we shall receive infinitely more than, supposing sin had never been, we should have received from Adam, a man deified.[3]

One cannot help feeling that there is a certain lack of reflection evident in such a passage. Certain questions immediately spring to mind. If the least of Christ's human acts was of infinite value why were we not redeemed by Christ's birth or a tear or a sigh? Why was there need for Jesus, a divine Person, to pass over from this world to the Father before atonement was made to God? Was it because God demanded in justice full retribution for sin, demanded, that is, the death of his Son? Is Christ's divinity a sufficient basis on its own account for the *representative* character of his life, death, and resurrection? In what sense and to what degree did the Son of God identify himself as man with us and our sinful condition? After all, did he not take upon himself our sin and our mortality?

(ii) *Jesus proved he was God by his miracles.* This was one of the major tenets of the older apologetics. Jesus claimed to be God and substantiated this claim by a series of extraordinary miracles.

The suggestion that Jesus went around claiming to be God is, to the mind of contemporary theologians and exegetes, over-simplified. For example, if we were to come across someone whom we witnessed working forty or fifty miracles which we could not explain, would we have to think of him as God, as necessarily and inevitably divine? We would probably ask him the question put to Jesus by the scribes and pharisees: "By whose authority do you do these things?"

It is true that Jesus professed himself to be in a unique relationship to God (the Father), an eternal relationship: he claimed to be the Son. But we cannot infer that every time Jesus accepted the title Son of God — he, in fact, always seems to have referred

---

[3] Jean Daujat, *The Theology of Grace* (London: Burns & Oates, 1959), p. 138.

to himself as Son of man — he accepted it as a token of belief in his divinity. "Son of God" was a messianic title like "Son of David." As such, it had no reference to his divinity. This is one instance among many where a more scientific exegesis of scripture has led to a different reading of certain texts and forced us to interpret the story of Christ's gradual revelation of himself to his disciples in a new way.

A further suggestion that Jesus proved he was God by working miracles displays a very rationalistic notion of faith, as if it were susceptible of proof. "Now faith is the assurance of things hoped for, the conviction of things not seen" (Heb 11:1). Christ, indeed, never worked miracles except in response to a faith that was already present. Faith, here, means faith in his word, in himself as God's messenger. The fact is that not even the apostles grasped his divinity and honored him as "the Lord" until the resurrection. The miracles were strange "proofs of divinity," then, when they did not even succeed in the case of Jesus' closest disciples. It would be to argue in an unusual manner were we to say that they were proofs of divinity after, and in the light of the resurrection — as if they became proofs when proofs were no longer necessary.

We should empty our heads once and for all of the idea that Christ proved his claim to be God by means of miracles. The miracles cannot be the basis of belief and it is only shallowness on our part which makes us wish that Jesus had worked his miracles in circumstances more adapted to verification! They were not supports of his teaching; they were part of his teaching, which was effective only on the supposition that his hearers believed in him. For those people who had committed themselves to him, for those who were so sensitized to God as to "receive" him as someone sent by God, his miracles were "signs." They showed to his sympathetic disciples what he meant to them: he was the healer of their blindness, their spiritual leprosy, their deafness; he was for them the resurrection and the life. In order to understand his wonders his hearers had first to yield themselves to him and then he was able to reveal to them his own special relationship to God. Their refusal to receive him was an indication that, despite their strict adherence to a ritualistic code of religion, in their hearts they were estranged from God. If they had known God they would have known Jesus, too.

Perhaps the worst result of considering Christ's miracles as proofs of his divinity was that they were considered to be the most significant episodes in our Lord's life. Yet greater than these wonderful signs was the sign of his death. It is less "wonderful" that God's Son should work miracles than that he should suffer agony and die. We in our obtuseness prefer to contemplate the miracles as pointers to God's power and love. They are more in keeping with our idea of God. But Christ did not come to confirm us in our idea of God; he came to give us a new idea of God on the basis of his own life, death, and resurrection. It is this newness against which we all rebel. We would much prefer a far less outrageous revelation of God (the Father) and of his love for us, one which allowed us simply to gape at the splendor of the divine fireworks. Suffering and serving love pursues us and haunts us; it will not leave us alone. God truly and irrevocably loves us in Christ and will not rest until he has converted us and won our hearts for himself.

In a word, a miracle does not show forth to us God as love as does Christ suffering and dying among us. A miracle, as it were, does not "tax" God so much or involve him so much. Now we see a further reason why Christ could not prove his case by miracles, for what he wanted to show, what he was determined to show, was that *God is love*, and this he demonstrated through the restricting circumstances of a human life and a human death. It was, therefore, not primarily what we call the "divine" in Christ's life that best shows forth his divinity (or oneness with the Father) but the human at its most human — when he was overwhelmed by sorrow, loneliness, and suffering, and when he succumbed to death.

In our foolishness we may even half-consciously suspect that if Christ had not worked any miracles we would not now believe in him. This is simply untrue. We believe in him because we experience him now as alive and revealing himself to us as once he revealed himself to his disciples. This is why his miracles speak to us. More, they speak better to us at this distant date than they spoke to those before whose eyes they were enacted. For we understand them in the light of the resurrection.

(iii) "Jesus proved he was God . . . *especially by the final miracle of raising himself from the dead.*" We have seen that it it wrong to think of Jesus as the greatest magician the world has ever known, ergo divine. Here we have simply to extend the principle. Jesus' resurrection does not "prove" his divinity either. The resurrection, a deed of the saving God, was no "Passover Plot."

The very way Peter speaks of Jesus on Pentecost day as being raised (note the passive voice) by God and made by him Lord and Christ (Acts 2:32, 36) shows that the prince of the apostles did not think of Jesus proving his own divinity by raising himself from death. After his crucifixion, Jesus manifested himself to his disciples as alive. They accepted him in faith, they who had followed him and loved him. Only those who had given their hearts to him were capable of seeing the risen Lord. This is our privilege, too. The older apologetics by stressing, as it were, the magic of the passing act of emergence from the tomb made us forget that the resurrection is a present reality. It means, in fact, that Jesus is among us as risen and alive by the power of the Spirit and that all men can meet him in faith.

The resurrection is not just a "proof" to convince men's minds but the very source of our Christian life. Indirectly, however, we see that it casts its light on Jesus' divinity insofar as by the resurrection God authenticates Christ's claim to be his Son. If God raised up Jesus to be "Lord (Yahweh's title in the Old Testament) and Christ," then everything that Jesus said and intimated about his relationship to his Father is true.

This is evidently not the same as considering the resurrection to be a proof of Christ's divinity. (This would be easier to grasp if we remembered that Jesus' resurrection really means Jesus' being raised from death, to a new and undying life.) Indeed, the resurrection ought not even to be thought or spoken of as a miracle at all. God's power is at work here but it cannot be called a miracle, for what is under discussion, Christ's being alive now whereas once he was dead, is not open to scientific investigation whatsoever. A miracle has surely some relationship to the empirical world. A happening at Lourdes, for example, is termed a miracle when a "before" and "after" in the world of experience can be compared; and the latter state is deemed to have no immediate causal connection with what went before. It can only have come about, believers say, by reason of some divine intervention, while unbelievers claim that it is due to some as yet undiagnosed physical factors. However, Jesus by his resurrection was removed from the eyes of the flesh (he was no longer open to empirical investigation) and made accessible only to the eyes of faith (he was present to those who, by faith, had already entered that world where he himself now dwells with his Father). The soldiers who guarded the tomb were the only ones to witness the "miracle" of a dead Christ mysteriously "leaving" the tomb: he was lying there and now he is there no longer. But it is not this witness of the soldiers that we have in mind when we speak of the early witness of the resurrection. The soldiers — and they alone — witnessed to the emptying of the tomb, but the apostles — and they alone — witnessed to the resurrection, that is, to the risen and living Christ. This they were able to do because they, unlike the guards at the tomb, had committed themselves to Jesus in faith.

Once more, the older apologetic, today's theologians suggest, is beside the point. Faith is not caused by acceptance of the emptiness of the tomb on Easter Sunday, a point which apologists once labored mightily to demonstrate. In fact, the soldiers who alone had experience of the actual emptying of the tomb did not believe at all. Rather, the mysterious episode of the empty tomb is itself accounted for by the conviction in faith that Jesus is alive. It is useless to base one's argument with unbelievers, therefore, on the fact that the tomb was empty when various people came and looked inside it. Unbelievers are bound

to have up their sleeve a score of explanations as to how this
could have happened. In order to account, in a way satisfactory
to Christians, for the empty tomb we have first to believe in
Jesus as alive, that is, to experience him here and now as a force
in my life. It is faith which accounts for the empty tomb, not
the empty tomb which produces faith.

This is exactly what the scriptures tell us happened in the
case of the apostles and the women. The empty tomb was to
them simply a source of disquiet and puzzlement until they
believed in the word of Jesus that he would rise from death.
When they met him, experienced him as alive, then they understood that the tomb was emptied by God's intervention and not
by someone stealing the body away. Apart from and independent
of faith the empty tomb will continue to be what it has, in fact,
always been in books written by rationalists, whether Christians
or non-Christians — an enormous red-herring.

God is revealed in Jesus' life history

A criticism of an earlier apologetic approach to Christ's divinity
and resurrection was necessary in order to introduce contemporary christology. The older emphasis on Christ's divinity, modern theologians argue, has led to a neglect of the history of
Christ's life, its development or unfolding. Apart from the unfolding of that human life, Jesus' divinity may be affirmed, but
it cannot be grasped as we were meant to grasp it. For the mystery
of the incarnation is that God is revealed in a new and final way
in the humanity and the life story of Jesus of Nazareth. It is
Jesus who, so to speak, gives content to "God" by revealing his
relationship to his Father throughout his earthly career. We get
to know more about God the more closely we watch and love
Jesus. To get a child of five to profess, "Jesus is God," is, therefore, in itself no triumph for religion. Until he has learned a

little about the man "Jesus" he doesn't know what he is talking about. Without Jesus we know neither God nor what perfect manhood consists in.

Once we begin to look on Jesus as truly a man on the march toward the fulfilment of his life, once we accept that his perfection lies not in the absence of struggle but in the ceaseless struggle to understand and to do God's will while surrounded by the forces of evil, then we can begin to identify ourselves in some measure with him. He is not simply "God-come-to-set-things-right." He is as much a man as we are. His divinity does not *replace* anything in Christ that is integral to true manhood. It is not as if the Word of God takes on some of the workings of Christ's human psyche, as if the divine person of the Son "plugs in," so to speak, to the electrical impulses in Christ's brain. That is perhaps the picture conjured up when we say Jesus is not a human person.

When we provide the full human context for our study of the incarnation, when we read the scriptures to search the face of Jesus the Man, we begin to realize that the resurrection was not simply a means of convincing us that Jesus is divine. It is the very consummation of Jesus as a man. It is the end and goal of his human development in this sinful world. He needed to be raised so as to be perfectly one with his Father. When, by the power of the Spirit, God raised him from death he gave to him, as a permanent possession, his own glory and an undying life. That glory and that life is ours to share. This is why without the resurrection we would all perish utterly.

The consciousness of Christ

All these facets of contemporary christology will be developed in Part II. The final question I want to raise here is that of Christ's consciousness. Today's theologians are quite prepared to admit that the Son as man was not omniscient. On the contrary, there were many things of which he was ignorant and toward an understanding of which he had to grope in the dark. Many theologians even speak of a true religious and spiritual development in Christ. Readers who are meeting these views for the first time are likely to be a little confused, even disturbed by them, so it is as well to make the following points clear. It is not suggested that Jesus only became God's Son in the course of his earthly career. What is under debate is only the human consciousness of Christ. The view being proposed is that Jesus, God's eternal Son, awoke gradually as man to self-awareness. He was immediately conscious of being God's Son and not just an ordinary man. Nonetheless, his awareness of being God's Son had to mature, become explicit, as time went on. He was able, as his mind developed, to verbalize and conceptualize better his unique relationship as Son to God his Father. Also, his consciousness of his Father's will presumably became clearer to him as his life progressed and especially as it drew to its close.

All this would seem to be entailed by Jesus' true humanity. Not that any one thinks it is possible to trace a consistent pattern of development in Christ's consciousness. Of Christ's early life we know almost nothing. In addition, his public ministry is presented to us in the scriptures as a gospel, a proclamation of the good news in the light of the resurrection and not as a standard biography. Only the exegete can tell us whether it is possible to work out some of the details of Christ's evolving consciousness. He will do so after examining thoroughly the accounts of Jesus' preaching, seeing whether there was any alteration in it as time went on. This is not a simple task because the exegete will have to decide how much of the text belongs to Christ's original preaching and how much has been elaborated by the evangelists and early teachers for the sake of their hearers. After all, the message of salvation had to be presented in a way accommodated to the needs of the audience. Even when the scholars have done their best it would seem that differences of opinion are likely to be considerable. All I would maintain here is that more important than the details is the general drift of modern christology, which is this: Jesus did truly grow in wisdom; he did need to pore over the scriptures (in fact, one of the best ways I know of reading the Old Testament is to read it as if one were Jesus seeking there an understanding of his mission in life); he did have to pick up the threads of his Father's will for him gradually, day by day; he did share with us something of our ignorance, our apprehension, our need to wait humbly and in patience.

None of this will lessen our respect for our divine Redeemer. Rather, it will endear him to us all the more, for we will feel closer kinship with him and appreciate far better the humiliation he endured by taking upon himself our slave-condition. It is by seeing how he reacted as man in that condition that we know how much God his Father loves us.

ORIGINAL SIN

I have deliberately chosen to write of Christ before original sin, of the second Adam before the first. This is because theologians and exegetes today concur in thinking that it is Christ who illuminates original sin and that the latter cannot be understood except in relation to him who came to take upon himself the sin of the world. "Who God is and what sin is, is fully revealed in Jesus Christ. His whole life was a revelation of God and at the same time a stand against sin. In and through confrontation with Jesus we gradually grow in our awareness of God's greatness and the abyss of sin. This is why the catechesis of Jesus Christ must dominate the whole of education in the faith."[4] It would seem to be a serious mistake, therefore, to attempt to teach small chil-

---

[4] *Fundamentals and Programs of a New Catechesis* by The Higher Institute of Catechetics of Nijmegen (Pittsburgh: Duquesne University Press, 1966), p. 131.

dren about the fall at a time when they cannot appreciate the gravity of sin either on the basis of their own experience or by deep meditation on Christ's passion. Most likely, they will take the story of Genesis with all its detail literally and have difficulties in faith later on when they become acquainted with the scientific origins of man and the universe.

The earlier approach to original sin

It is not only children's books which give the impression that Genesis records an eyewitness account of the events in Eden. Let us instance Leo J. Trese's *The Faith Explained*.[5] The author tells us that God gave Adam and Eve a single commandment to keep; obedience to such a commandment was the necessary proof of their love. He writes: "They must not eat of the fruit that grew on a certain tree. It probably was no different (except in its effects) from any of the other fruits which Adam and Eve could reach out and pick."[6] The notion of God imposing an arbitrary restriction on the freedom of Adam and Eve and prohibiting them from eating the fruit of a particular tree is too ingenuous by far to criticize. The author continues with the over optimistic comment on why we must suffer when we did not personally commit original sin. "*With a moment's thought, the question answers itself. We have not lost, any of us, anything which we are by right entitled to.*"[7] (Italics mine.) Father Trese then gives the example of someone whose father refused the offer of a million dollars in exchange for some small service before he was born. What right, in the strict sense, has the son to complain?

This kind of writing is an illustration of what happens when a skilled popularizer handles outdated material. The attempt at

---

[5] Fides, 1963.
[6] *Loc. cit.*, p. 53.
[7] *Ibid.*, p. 56.

popularization merely reveals the shallowness and dangers of the underlying theology.

A similarly unnuanced presentation is to be found in an even more recent work, *Roman Catholicism*.[8] Here we read:

> God created Adam out of nothing and fashioned Eve from his body. The human race has descended from them as its sole parents. . . .
> They each had an immaterial soul created in the image and likeness of God (Gen 1:27; 2:7). Each had the natural gift proper to human nature, such as the use of Reason, and also Supernatural Gifts, such as the state of Grace, to enable them to attain their supernatural end of possessing God in heaven. Additionally they had preternatural gifts added to human nature: although they could die, for instance, they would not in fact have done so had they remained in the state of union with God in which they were created.[9]

Several points of interest arise from this passage. Genesis is interpreted literally as to the descent of the human race from a single pair. At the same time Adam is said to have been created *out of nothing*, no mention being made of the Genesis picture of Adam being formed out of the slime of the earth or of any evolutionary possibilities. Adam and Eve are said to have had *an immaterial soul* created in God's image and we are asked to consult two passages in Genesis which, in effect, do not refer to man's soul at all but to man becoming by God's breath a *living being*. The Bible never divides man up into the two compartments of body and soul as this author does. This explains why a little later in *Roman Catholicism* we read these startling remarks on infants descended from Adam. "When God created their souls, inevitably in grace and holiness, their innocence was tainted and destroyed when soul and diseased nature were united."[10] Here, "diseased nature" can only be taken to mean "body." Furthermore, in the long passage quoted above, the state of grace is spoken of as simply a means by which people get to heaven. What grace is in itself, whether it is something more

---

[8] By David Quinlan, London, 1966.
[9] *Loc. cit.*, p. 29.
[10] *Ibid.*, p. 31.

than just a means to final beatitude is not stated. Finally. Adam and Eve are said to have possessed preternatural gifts, one of which was the gift of immortality. God promised Adam and Eve that in fact they would not die.

More than twenty five years ago C. S. Lewis in his book, *The Problem of Pain*,[11] made a far finer and more heroic effort to render the traditional approach to the fall intellectually respectable. "The gravitation away from God," he wrote, " 'the journey homeward to habitual self,' must, we think, be a product of the Fall."[12] He went on to give an account of how the fall may have happened. Man was once all consciousness. The first member (or members) of the race had even organic processes under the control of his will. (Some Yogis today claim to have a limited control in this area.) By reason of man's command of organic processes "it may not be fanciful to suppose that the length of his life was largely at his own discretion. Wholly commanding himself, he commanded all lower lives with which he came into contact. Even now we meet rare individuals who have a mysterious power of taming beasts. This power the Paradisal man enjoyed in eminence. The old picture of the brutes sporting before Adam and fawning upon him may not be wholly symbolical."[13]

C. S. Lewis thought that in terms of language and the things he was able to make the first man was no doubt a savage, clumsy and unpracticed. Perhaps, too, like a small child he was capable of undergoing profound spiritual experiences while still being unable to express them in conceptual form. Then came a time when man stood in opposition to God. Such opposition was necessarily some act of the human will which constituted "an utter falseness to its true creaturely position." This was the fall, a particularly heinous crime in that the first man was not tempted as we are; he had "no passion or inclination obstinately inclining that way — nothing but the bare fact that the self was *himself*."

---

[11] The Centenary Press, 1941.
[12] *Loc. cit.*, p. 64.
[13] *Ibid.*, p. 66.

The spirit's full control of the human organism was lost because the spirit, once in harmony with God, was now in revolt against him. Man's mind was weakened, his will no longer dominant. Pain, senility, and death came in. C. S. Lewis wrote: "The process was not, I conceive, comparable to mere deterioration as it may now occur in a human individual; it was a loss of status as a species. What man lost by the Fall was his original specific nature."[14] A new kind of man had, therefore, emerged; "a new species, never made by God, had sinned itself into existence." The present situation can only be called original sin. This is still preferable, according to C. S. Lewis, to original misfortune. A child who grows up vicious because, when small, he was deprived of love is truly vicious. His character, however much we sympathize with him, is correctly termed detestable and not merely a misfortune. Likewise man as we now know him to be is as he is by reason of factors beyond his present control; and yet we have no choice but to speak of him as being sinful.

Doubts about the earlier approach

Because of the very brilliance of C. S. Lewis' "Socratic myth" the modern reader is probably more puzzled than ever by the Christian doctrine of original sin. If such brilliance is needed to make the customary teaching on original sin remotely interesting let alone intellectually satisfying, might there not be something wrong with the customary teaching? Is it really necessary or even possible today to believe that there were such extraordinary beings at the origin of the race? Is there not something a little whimsical in the thought of their being immune from pain, senility, and death; in their being all consciousness; in their will's dominance over the decay and repair of bodily tissues; in their ability to determine the length of their days; in their wholly amicable

---

[14] *Ibid.*, p. 70.

relations with the brute creation? Despite Lewis' qualifications whereby the more obvious absurdities in some of the older presentations of original sin — still current, as I have shown, in some circles — are avoided, the question arises: Is not this whole project of trying to make the traditional theology respectable unrealistic? Does this same traditional theology fit in with today's refined exegesis of scripture and with the new scientific picture of man's origin? Are we perhaps trying to patch up an old edifice when complete demolition and rebuilding are called for?

Many contemporary authors are prepared to say that original sin — the condition into which all men are born, the condition in which they cannot reach God without divine help — can and should be examined without necessarily resorting to a single couple at the roots of the race who were causally responsible for this condition. Even when Adam and Eve are still mentioned their significance and stature are patently not what they were. For example, Piet Smulders, S.J., writes: "Scripture and the Church teach that Adam was preserved from the *brutal* death, alone deserving of the name, which is a punishment for sin. They seem to make no pronouncement about death as our natural end. Apparently we are not obliged to picture man in paradise as utterly preserved from the law of decay which awaits every organism living on earth."[15] A few further examples will make plain the general position of the authors whose views I am trying to describe.

A new approach to original sin

In *Fundamentals and Programs of a New Catechesis* we read: "The situation, in virtue of which man cannot begin with himself and from his own existence but must depend upon grace that comes from the saving Christ, is traditionally called 'original

---

[15] *Theology Digest* (Autumn, 1965), p. 176.

sin.' "[16] Later the fall of man is described as "an image of the disrupted world in which we now live."[17]

Rosemary Haughton in her book, *On Trying to be Human*,[18] first speaks of the sad inability of men to understand themselves and to communicate with others, of the web of fear we weave about ourselves, of the complex and multitudinous defense-mechanisms we erect in our efforts to achieve quietude and immunity from pain. Then she continues:

> All this is covered by the term "original sin." Divorced from the state it indicates, given an independent being of its own, it is used not merely to describe but to explain. It acquires implications of guilt, and since the condition of original sin is common to every individual human being from conception, at which point he is obviously not guilty of anything at all, it is thought of as being transmitted in the process of generation, not (as it must be) simply because that is how human beings are, but as if it were an extra "something" — "stain" is the word most often used — which was handed down from the first pair, who were actually personally "guilty," to all those who were not but who were thereby condemned to suffer the condition incurred by their progenitors. But as long as the phrase is purely descriptive it does very well. As long as we ask *what* and not *why*, "original sin" is a good enough answer. It refers to an experienced and verifiable condition in which we feel and know that there is "something wrong."[19]

It is the total *lack of relevance* and the excessive *simplifications* of the traditional picture of original sin that most modern authors object to. How is it possible, they ask, to describe the alleged sin of our progenitors, so disastrous in its consequences, as becoming in us "a stain upon the soul"? What is the strange spiritual-corporeal mechanism whereby this deadly stain is handed on from parents to children and yet is "washed away" completely should the child happen to be numbered among those favored few who are baptized?

The attempt is being made by theologians to widen on all fronts our conception of sin which has been too juridical at times;

---

[16] *Fundamentals and Programs of a New Catechesis*, p. 94.
[17] *Ibid.*, p. 239.
[18] Templegate, 1966.
[19] *Loc. cit.*, p. 24.

to show the relationship between personal sin and the sin which is our inheritance; to bring out the many forces which can influence each new member of the race for the worse — education, family, environment and so on. There is a kind of accumulation of inherited defects in the course of the ages which we all know to be both wrong and inevitable. Confronted by this "sin of the world" we acknowledge our total helplessness. In this context the words of Louis Monden, S.J., are apposite:

> It is a striking fact that Catholic dogmatic theology is becoming more and more inclined to conceive original sin as a *situation* brought about in mankind from the very beginning, an initial option which keeps spreading more widely as mankind expands and growing stronger with the individual sins of each person. On the other hand, each man, even before he is able to use his freedom, is by the very fact of being historically situated within mankind unavoidably caught up in the sphere of influence of that evil, as an area of darkness which he cannot conquer by his own power and which holds him back from the meeting with God. Men have first become fully aware of this general situation of sinfulness in their rejection of Christ . . . in this view, original sin would not be some kind of juridical imputation of a past event, but a situation which continues to exert its effects, and to be accepted and confirmed by every personal sin.[20]

The authors quoted in this section are certainly more sophisticated than those quoted in the previous section. The problem is: Does orthodoxy demand that we assert still a single couple at the beginning of the race, specially endowed with bodily prerogatives and living in the radiant glow of a special divine friendship? Are we not bound to affirm that sin is handed on from parents to children by the process of generation? How do the contemporary theologians who are so impressed by the findings of modern science harmonize their own teaching with that of St. Paul or the Council of Trent? What are we to say of their integration into theology of a dynamic conception of the universe whereby sin is measured not so much by reference to a lost Eden of the past but to mankind's stubborn, age-long refusal to cooperate with Christ in building up God's kingdom on earth? Is it possible

---

[20] *Sin, Liberty and Law* (New York: Sheed & Ward, 1966), p. 72.

to agree with Smulders and others that it was not biological death which came into the world as the wages of sin but the anguished, brutal death such as we know it?

These are some of the questions which will be taken up in Part III in a more academic and satisfying fashion than is possible in this brief introduction.

Enough has been said, I hope, to convince the reader that the two issues chosen for discussion here are both important and interesting. They are not easy to resolve. They will be debated for a long time to come.

PART II

The incarnation

Theology is the study of a man

Theology (the science of God) is the science of a Man, Jesus
Christ. This is the paradox of our faith and it is well to begin
this study with it. All subsequent theological reflection takes its
origin here.

Someone might object: A more adequate statement would be
that theology is the science of the God-Man, Jesus Christ. In a
sense, this is true; but strangely enough this more adequate
formulation may hide from us the startling and unique emphasis
of the Christian message. It is in and through the human life
story of Jesus that God is manifested and makes his decisive
entrance into the world.

God dwells in inaccessible light. He becomes knowable insofar as he manifests himself by acts (or events) and words; by
what he does for us and what he tells us. Indeed, his very acts
are words (or teaching) and his words are actions. He saves
both when he intervenes in history, say, in the passover of the

Jews from bondage in Egypt to the promised land, and also when
he speaks through the mouths of the prophets.

This God who manifested himself throughout Jewish history
as "the God who saves" has manifested himself above all in Jesus
of Nazareth. It is in the story of this Man living among men
that God has finally and fully become known. Jesus is the first
Word of God who has become flesh, and so, in a rather different
sense, the last word of God to men. Christ's life, however, if it
is to convey to us the plenary reality of God, must be looked at
as a whole. From his birth until his presence (or *parousia*) in
glory we are dealing with the single coming of God's only Son.

If God has done everything he will ever do for us and told
us everything he will ever tell us in Christ it should be evident
that we must put Christ at the center of all our teaching. When
we forget him for a moment it is as if a cold, winter wind comes
off the sea and blows through all our lessons. What we say of
God and religious things evaporates in an air of unreality.

The neglect of Christ

"Christ in all our teaching." It is an easy slogan to mouth
and to remember. How appallingly difficult to make much of it
in practice. Why is this?

It is at least partly due to the textbooks of an earlier period
against which there has been such a strong reaction in recent
years. So often they gave us the impression that they had dealt
exhaustively with God's revelation or at least some aspects of it.
This was very strange in that many of these books, when dealing
with the subject of revelation, made use of but a few selected
texts which were apportioned to particular "theses" to be proved
very much as a pack of cards is distributed among the players
in a game.

The statements of the Council of Chalcedon on the incarnation were often quoted as if the whole matter ended there. All that Christians had to do was learn them and "believe" them to be true. Fortunately, things are not so easy as that — and much more enriching. As Karl Rahner has remarked: "It follows from the nature of human knowledge of truth and from the nature of divine truth itself, that any individual truth, above all one of God's truths, is beginning and emergence, not conclusion and end. In the last resort any individual human perception of truth only has meaning as beginning and promise of the knowledge of God."[1]

Another reason why it is difficult to focus all our teaching on Christ is that there are whole tracts of theology in the ordinary manuals and the catechisms based on them into which Christ hardly enters at all. While theologians — biblical theologians for the most part — have struggled hard to remedy this, the emendations made in the manuals have been slight. It could be that the manual itself as a literary genre will not be of much use to our generation.

When we turn, for instance, to these manuals and look up the treatise on what are called the theological virtues of faith, hope and charity, Christ who is God's Son, his Word (or perfect Image) may not even be mentioned. And yet he said such things as: "This is the will of my Father, that every one who sees the Son and *believes in him* should have eternal life" (Jn 6:40; cf. 11:25).

In the manuals, sin is treated only as something from which Christ redeems us, whereas in the New Testament it is of the very nature of sin to be a rejection of Christ, a refusal to believe in him. In the manuals, grace is referred to as the grace of Christ, since he won it for us, whereas the New Testament presents grace as life in Christ, an abiding in him (Jn 6:56; 15:4), a sharing in his relationship to the Father. In each case the scriptures seem to be moving at a far deeper level than speculative theology.

Perhaps the place in the manuals where we become most conscious of the absence of Christ is in the tracts on the "last things,"

---

[1] *Theological Investigations* (Baltimore: Helicon, 1961), Vol. 1, p. 149.

death, purgatory, judgment, hell, and heaven. Here if anywhere, we are inclined to think, Jesus should figure prominently. But he does not. Let us instance heaven. John Calvin thought it probable that Christ at the judgment will put off his humanity so as to show forth his divinity in all its glory. The manuals rightly deny such an idea, yet give little or no indication of what is the real role of Christ's humanity in our heavenly blessedness.

Surely the scriptures show us that the Son became man to lead us in that manhood to God, and by that same manhood to reveal God to us even in heaven. This is why the first Christians so longed for the coming of Jesus from heaven, for everlasting joy without him is unthinkable. "It is the God who said, 'Let light shine out of darkness' who has shone in our hearts to give the light of the knowledge of the glory of God in the face of Christ" (2 Cor 4:6). When Christ comes for us, he will say what he said to Philip when he walked the earth: "He who has seen me has seen the Father" (Jn 14:9).

How unreal our presentation of heaven became as a result of our neglect of Christ and our lack of emphasis on resurrection. Our post-mortem bliss has been depicted as essentially that of souls gazing on the naked glory of the invisible God, so that we were in danger of having this dreadful situation on our hands: promising youngsters, at the end of their lifelong labors, a reward which exercised no hold upon their minds and imaginations and which none of them wanted. Evidently, we must bring into greater prominence the cardinal doctrines of the Catholic faith: the resurrection of Christ (that is, the everlasting bodiliness, mediation, and priesthood of the Word); our own bodily resurrection; heaven as the society or fellowship of the risen who have committed themselves to God *through Christ* for ever. These doctrines are written large in the New Testament, and recent theologians — unhappily referred to as proponents of a "new theology" — have simply reminded us of their central position in the presentation of the gospel message.[2]

---

[2] See Gabriel Moran, *Theology of Revelation* (New York: Herder & Herder, 1966), pp. 184–185.

The last area of theology we shall mention — and a large one at that — in which Christ has been conspicuous by his absence is moral theology. Until recently moral theology had cut its moorings to the gospel message: it had become very little else than an expanded and updated version of Aristotle's *Ethics* with a seasoning of religious exhortation ("Do this out of love of Christ") and a promise of grace to fortify us in our endeavors. Paul, by contrast, relates all his moral teaching to Christ's death and resurrection and therefore to baptism which is the means by which the Christian shares in the reality of that twofold event.

It is only too easy to criticize the past and forget our debt to those who have gone before us. It is only too easy to term "revolutionary" changes which earlier ages would have accepted as quite normal. On the one hand, then, let us remember that authors whom we feel bound to criticize defended the faith with a vigor and success we cannot match. On the other hand, we may feel called upon in all sincerity to go back further in history than they to recover a more balanced and less controversial presentation of the Christian message. This is not a new theology but a renewal of theology often made possible by remembering long-forgotten things. For some years we have seen stirrings and signs of such a renewal in every branch of the sacred sciences, in moral theology as well which is now more correctly seen to be a theology of morals. And theology, as we saw, is the study of this Man Jesus, who is called 'Christ."

Practical unbelief in Christ's humanity

If it is asked why Christ was for so long given a small place in certain theological tracts the answer can only be: because of the practical unbelief in Christ's humanity. Those who, on the level of credal profession, would not dream of denying that Jesus is a man will need some convincing that there lurks in all of us a reluctance to accept the full reality of Jesus' manhood.

When Dorothy L. Sayers' famous plays *The Man Born to Be King* were first performed on the radio in 1941 strong protests came from certain quarters. Mr. J. W. Welch, then Director of Religious Broadcasting B.B.C., had this to say of the dissidents:

> The disturbing feature of the opposition was its revelation of a widespread and seriously defective theology of the Incarnation. "The Word was made flesh" — how many of us dare believe that? Some listeners were quite incapable of believing that Christ laughed, said "good morning," or was in any sense fully *human*; and even supporters of the plays flinched and shrank from the glimpse of the Crucifixion we were given in the eleventh play. There is so much "cotton-wool" between us and what really happened that many of us are *now incapable of listening* to the true story of Christ. We *dare* not "behold the Man"; we dare only behold our easy and comfortable version of him. Is this reverence? Is it not, rather, the *main* reason why the Gospel story does not arrest, convict, attract, compel men to a decision? I must humbly confess that these plays revealed the poverty and incompleteness of my own belief in the Incarnation. Again and again when the figure of Christ in these plays faced one with a direct challenge one's reaction was "No! not that, anything but that!" The Christ in these plays is, for any who are prepared to read them *and think*, a veritable Hound of Heaven. The eleventh play, on the Crucifixion, though it only hinted at the physical horror we were spared, was almost unbearable because the stupidity and brutality of the ordinary man and woman in the crowd convicted us. *We don't want to believe* that the Crucifixion was like *that*.[3]

Each one of us, if he looks into his heart searchingly, will probably feel compelled to admit with J. W. Welch "the poverty and incompleteness of my own belief in the incarnation."

The way we have been taught about Christ in catechisms and the like is responsible for this. The approach has been: Jesus is divine, that is the important thing; Jesus is also human, that is evidently very important too in that he is our savior, our priest and mediator. But what teachers rush to tell their children is, "Jesus is God." I had a remarkable instance of this recently when teaching a group of children about the death and resurrection of Jesus with the help of a home-made Easter sepulchre.

---

[3] *The Man Born to Be King*, Foreword (London: 1953), p. 16.

I asked one boy of six: "Who is Jesus?" Before he could reply another little fellow aged five, who had been at school only a month and a half, interjected: "He's God." No doubt, his teacher had considered this the first truth he had to be taught. How much better to have taught him about Jesus of Nazareth who is God's only Son. Gradually, as he came to see the extraordinarily kind and gentle love of the Father, he would realize more and more in a concrete and living way the uniqueness of Christ's filial relationship to God. This, after all, was Christ's own way with his apostles. The time for formalizing our faith should come later in a child's education when such formulization is necessary.

Non-Catholics, we believe — and sometimes correctly — are not always very clear and emphatic enough about Christ's divinity. So we bang down hard on the other side of the balance and thunder forth: "Jesus is God!" And Christ's manhood may very well slip from view. We can even divide Christ up in this way. "Jesus is God" — primary truth. "Jesus is man" — secondary truth and *in comparison unimportant*. This is to forget that Christ's divinity is not merely a subject of affirmation but of exploration. We need to know not only that Jesus is God but what divinity is, what God is like *for us*.

Everything the Man of Nazareth says and does is a revelation of God. God is at work among us in Jesus. He reveals himself in the living and dying of a member of the human race.

"Jesus is God." Has this cry made our ears completely insensitive to all the other acclamations in the New Testament? Have we forgotten that after his resurrection Jesus is acclaimed as alive, the Lord, Christ? With the aid of attested authors of our day, we shall attempt to answer these questions under the following major headings:

   (i)   The profession, "Jesus is God," has immobilized our theology.

   (ii)   The profession, "Jesus is God," is used to evacuate areas of Christ's humanity.

   (iii)   The profession, "Jesus is God," can lead to a practical neglect of the Trinity.

(i)   *The profession, "Jesus is God," has immobilized our theology*

We must strain — contrary, it may be, to the religious formation we have received — to see Christ's life as a fully human life.
It is an historical life, with movement in it, with a "becoming"
or progression in it toward a fulfilment. I am referring here to
the fulfilment of *his life*, not simply to the accomplishment of
our salvation. In fact, it is dangerous to separate these two things.
Christ's coming to his human fulfilment *is* our salvation.

I have spoken of Jesus "becoming" something. This is important in that it focuses our gaze on Christ's humanity. "Becoming"
is not a property of divinity.

If Jesus is God's eternal Son become man what more can he
become? Lord and Christ by resurrection. Does this mean that
before his resurrection Jesus was not yet Lord and Christ? Not
in the fullest sense any way. Jesus of Nazareth was a man attested
by God "with mighty works and wonders and signs" (Acts 2:22),
and Peter tells the Jews of Jerusalem on Pentecost day: "Let all
the house of Israel therefore know assuredly that God *has made
him* both Lord and Christ, this Jesus whom you crucified" (Acts
2:36).

Evidently, the profession of faith "Jesus is God" does not mark
the end of theology. We cannot, having made it, close the scriptures and say, "Here, in this assertion, is the distilled essence of
the Bible." To do this is equivalent to a denial of the incarnation,
for what engages our faith in this mystery is not that God should
be God (the Transcendent) but that God's eternal Son should
be a man.

It is only too easy to treat Jesus as a man temporarily dwelt
in by God. Again, it must be emphasized, we are dealing not
with the level of credal profession but of practical response. Our
unbelief in the full reality of Christ's manhood is implicit rather
than explicit. For example, we claim: "When Jesus died on the
cross for us we were redeemed. That death was important because it is the death of God. Hence the infinite worth of it."

While agreeing with the general content of these remarks, we are bound to point out that there is only a half truth expressed there. Every act of Christ, being the act of a divine person, is of infinite value, so that if special emphasis is put, in scripture, on the death (and resurrection) of Jesus something more than "value" is under consideration. What is this something more? It can only be the role of Christ's death in the structure of our redemption. The New Testament is not concerned directly with the infinite value (or merits) of Christ, which is a rather hellenic and abstract conception. It is concerned with events, with what happened to Christ. These events are of immediate interest not for the graces they "won" but in and for themselves. The questions uppermost in the minds of the New Testament writers are, What was the importance of Christ's death for *Christ?* and, What did Christ become by reason of his death? — for had Christ died and not been raised, however infinite the merits of that death, our faith would be futile and we would still be in our sins (1 Cor 15:17). Only when the answers to these questions are found are we in a position to understand what value the death of Christ had for us.

Once more our reflections summon us back to a deeper investigation of Christ's humanity. The scholastic expression, "Christ's humanity is the instrument of the Word" does not help us in this and, it might be argued, is more than dangerous in our day. It inevitably gives our contemporaries the impression that Christ's manhood is something used *by* the Lord and something disposable afterwards as is a paint brush when an artist has finished the painting he was engaged on. It is an expression that encourages us to look at the incarnation as God at work in the world and, as it were, utilizing a man for his purposes. We, on the contrary, believing that Jesus is not a man dwelt in by God, not even a perfect man dwelt in by God, want to center upon Jesus who was born in Bethlehem, brought up in Nazareth and who walked the roads in Galilee. We want to avoid any expressions that make it seem as if Jesus is a kind of puppet manipulated by the Word of God in his determination to redeem the human race.

The teaching of scripture

God's Son is a man for ever, someone who, when he walked the earth, was on the move, so to speak; he was called to make decisions and to learn obedience by suffering, called to endure in our humanity a condition of distance or exile from God.

Today's theologians realize sympathetically that such a notion does not come easily to Christians whose religious education has emphasized almost exclusively the divinity of Christ. Yet can there be any doubt about the message of scripture? Even the Fourth Gospel, which is the clearest of all in its confession of the divinity of Jesus, does not let us forget that Jesus is, through incarnation, away from his Father and needing to pass over to him by means of death. For John the Evangelist the passover of Jesus from this world to the Father is the final phase of the movement of his life, a passover which was foreshadowed by the passover of Christ's own people, the Jews, from the bondage of Egypt into the land of promise. Christ, then, like the Jews, had first to endure a condition of exile and slavery before he could reach his Father.

What John represents in terms of a geographical movement, St. Paul speaks of in terms of Christ being first in the flesh and next, at resurrection, in the Spirit. Paul means that Christ in his humility came into a world in which sin, death, and the law were in command. Christ the holy, sinless One of God "emptied himself" into this sin-laden condition of ours. It is worth noting that it is not of itself a humiliation or a self-emptying for God's Son to be a man — for he is a man for ever and yet not humiliated for ever by reason of this. The humiliation comes from the Son being a man in the present godless condition of manhood which is the consequence of the sin of the world. In fact, Jesus took on himself this sin of the world, this state of alienation from God. This is his self-emptying. This is why when he died upon the cross he is spoken of by Paul as becoming a curse, being made sin for our sakes. He died the death of our sins.

Current theology has highlighted these statements of Paul. Earlier, Jesus' personal sinlessness was always to the fore — it is significant that Jesus, so outraged by pharisaism, never once asks the Father for forgiveness — whereas his identification with us in our sinful condition was more or less neglected. Both aspects need to be considered together for they complement one another. Jesus is the sinless One in our sinful state, the perfect Man in our imperfect condition.

This alone accounts for some otherwise inexplicable and certainly forceful texts in the New Testament which cannot be left aside without the loss of one of the richest aspects of the mystery of Christ. Let us recall some of these texts with but the briefest commentary on them.

Jesus looks forward to his death and resurrection because then he will be with his Father. This event he speaks of as his "baptism" (Lk 12:50, Mk 10:38–39). He knows he needs to be cleansed of our sinful condition by his death. Hence he prayed to God at the Supper: "For their (the apostles') sake I consecrate (or sanctify) myself" (Jn 17:19).

Likewise at the Supper Jesus prays to be "glorified." "Now, Father, glorify thou me with the glory which I had with thee before the world was made" (Jn 17:5). John sees Christ upon the cross as glorified or exalted, simultaneously lifted up in ignominy before men's eyes and into the glory to his Father (Jn 12:24). It is only at the end of his life, then, that Jesus receives into his humanity the fulness of the glory of God which was his by rights and which he possessed in his divine nature before the world was made.

The Acts of the Apostles speak of Jesus, as we noted, becoming Lord and Christ, Kyrios and Christos, by his resurrection (2:36). Later, Jesus is spoken of as being exalted at God's right hand "as Leader and Savior" after having been hanged upon a tree (5:30–31). What is brought out here is that salvation comes about through the saving God of the Old Testament exercising his influence upon Jesus, so that he becomes the Christ, the one in whom mankind is reconciled to God and who is the fullest and most literal embodiment of God's salvific action. In a word, salvation is in Christ. Jesus risen is the site of all God's saving and sanctifying influence. John expressed this by saying that it is the risen and glorified Christ who gives the Spirit of life and holiness. Before then Jesus' flesh was of no avail unto salvation (cf. Jn 7:39, 6:63).

Paul sees the resurrection as Christ's new birth when he receives his new name, Jesus the Lord (Phil 2:9–11). He thinks of him as needing to put off our state of weakness in order to assume the power which is his by right. He "was descended from David according to the flesh (i.e., the state of weakness, pain, mortality) and constituted the Son of God in power according to the Spirit of holiness by his resurrection from the dead, Jesus Christ our Lord" (Rom 1:4). The Apostle even sees Christ's resurrection as his being justified: "He was manifested in the flesh, justified in the Spirit" (1 Tim 3:16). The Epistle to the Colossians speaks of the fulness of God being pleased to dwell in Christ since he is the firstborn from the dead (Col 1:18–19).

Finally, in this brief outline of scripture texts we can mention the Epistle to the Hebrews. The author applies the second verse of Psalm 2, "Thou art my Son, today I have begotten thee" to Christ on the day of his glorification or ascension (Heb 1:5). He also refers to the passion of Christ as *perfecting* him. It was only when Jesus was made perfect that he became the source of eternal salvation to all who obey him (Heb 5:9).

The growing reality of Christ's life

The scriptures make us realize very forcefully the truly human quality of Christ's life, the drama of it, what I have called the "movement" of it, the movement whose final phase is Christ's passage to his Father. As Father Durrwell puts it: Jesus was God's Son, but there were within him quite considerable elements which God's glorifying holiness did not enter; not only his body, but all the faculties which brought him into contact with us, were so incompletely possessed by the life of God that Christ could suffer fear and anguish, that the Son of the immortal God could succumb to death.[4]

Christ is not God in fancy dress. He has shared with us, in his sinlessness, the condition of an unredeemed world. This is why he reached out, especially toward the end, to the "other world"; this is why he longed to go home to his Father, to put off this present condition of the flesh in which he humbly walked for our sakes. It would seem legitimate to depict Christ in our teaching as a son wanting to go home, even as a little child longing to be welcomed into the joy and security of his Father's house. Or depict him as a refugee or an exile desirous of returning to the land of his birth.

Scripture reveals to us the growing quality of Christ's human existence. Father Schillebeeckx, O.P. has put it like this:

> The incarnation of the Son of God is a reality which grows. It is not complete in a matter of a moment; for example, at Jesus' conception in Mary's womb or at his birth. The incarnation is not merely a Christmas event. To be man is a process of becoming man; Jesus' manhood grew throughout his earthly life, finding its completion in the supreme moment of the incarnation, his death, resurrection and exaltation.[5]

It is only too easy to argue that since "Jesus is God" he is perfect in every sense from the beginning of his earthly career. In one sense, naturally, it is true that Jesus is perfect. How could he have revealed God perfectly if he were not perfect himself in his response to God? How could an unloving Christ have revealed a loving God? But Christ suffered from what I have called — and I have labored this point because it seems to me to be so frequently neglected — our imperfect condition. In this condition, he was not fully at one with God, even though he gave himself to God always in utter obedience and wholehearted

---

[4] *In the Redeeming Christ* (New York: Sheed & Ward, 1963), p. 6.
[5] *Christ the Sacrament of the Encounter With God* (New York: Sheed & Ward, 1963), p. 20.

love. Moreover, suffering the unredeemed condition of mankind
he was not perfectly one with us either. He was himself the
grain of wheat *alone* until he died. He was, to use a paradoxical
expression, one with us in our disunity until he became the firstborn of many brethren by reason of his resurrection. In fact,
here we have come to the very core of Christ's agony on earth.
This was not the physical torment, as we know. His agony was
caused by his inability to give to his fellow men the Spirit of
love and union (cf. Jn 7:39). He had to die to bring men into
one. For though he possessed the Spirit at birth, and though
the Spirit rested and remained on him at the inauguration of
his public life when he was baptized in the Jordan, he needed
a further baptism in the Spirit, the baptism of death. It was
when he died that he sent or "breathed forth" the Spirit upon
the world. Then, too, his heart was pierced so that the water —
which in the Old Testament often stood for God's holy Spirit —
washed his body and became available to the parched souls of
men. Indeed, Jesus is the rock in the desert of man's earthly
life stricken by the soldier's lance and irrigating the wilderness.

The point is that only when Jesus is glorified, "spiritualized"
in death can the Spirit be released. This shows the humiliation
Christ endured for our sakes in accepting the slave-condition of
mortal men. It shows, too, how truly human Jesus is. He took
into himself our very condition of separation from God which
reached its highest point at the moment of death. What this
demanded of him we can only dimly visualize.

We put up with the condition of this world convinced that
Jesus has triumphed over its godlessness, taken the poison out of
it. We bear the pain of it in company with Jesus our Lord and
King. The very meaning of sorrow, anguish, and death is changed
for us now. Our world is a redeemed world. Our pain, loneliness,
and death are always, as it were, diluted and sweetened by the
redeeming Christ. Jesus alone bore sin alone, whereas we are
never alone — or need not be — in that faith joins us to him as
he now is, triumphant and risen. For us, the devastating solitude
of sin is over. Jesus died to sin on the cross. In a world of dis-

obedience, he was perfectly obedient; in a loveless world, his was a flawless love.

The doctrine of atonement

It is the obedience and love of Christ which is the key to the doctrine of atonement. How easy it is to present God the Father as demanding justice, his pound of flesh in Shylock fashion. Even Hans Urs von Balthasar speaks of Christ reaching "the abyss between the flaming, raging justice of God and man 'abandoned' and rejected by him."[6] Is it not misleading and dangerous to speak of the atonement in such terms? What is intended by them — the radical opposition between God's holiness and man's sinfulness (cf. Rom 1:18) — is correct, but what is conveyed by them is often a very false, irate picture of God. Scripture means by "God's wrath," according to Bultmann, an occurence, namely, the judgment of God, whereas we are too easily prone to take it as a quality, an emotion, the wrathfulness of God. God sends his Son because he loves us and not because he is wrathful or hypersensitive about the demands of his justice. It is only an imperfect understanding of the incarnation which could lead to this rigid, and now widely rejected idea of atonement. Let me explain what I mean.

If we look at Jesus simply in cold, still, metaphysical terms as divine and human we may well wonder what more is to be done after Jesus was conceived in Mary's womb. If sin is the cleavage between God and men then why was this cleavage not healed when the Son became man? In his own person has not Christ united perfectly the two parties until then separated from one another? Was not Christ's mediation complete when Mary said: "Behold the handmaid of the Lord"?

We know it was not, but why was it not complete then? Was

---

[6] *A Theology of History* (New York: Sheed & Ward, 1963), p. 64.

it because God's justice had not yet been sated? Was it because he still demanded a death of atonement before he would agree that the scales of justice had been rightly balanced? In such a perspective Jesus' terrible death upon the cross reveals primarily the divine justice, that "flaming, raging justice" to which Von Balthasar referred.

All this would seem contrary to what the scriptures tell us. The crucifixion was not demanded by God but by men. It does not reveal God's justice in the strict juridical sense but man's injustice.[7] It is the *love* of God which is expressed in Jesus' dying upon the cross. For Jesus is the sacrament of God; his love for men *is* God's love for men.

The cleavage between men and God was opened up by men. God remains unalterable in his love. The atonement is to be looked at as God in his merciful love sending his Son not to restore the balance of justice but to express a perfect love for him such as mankind had hitherto been unwilling or unable to give. The atonement is a work of divine sensitivity, not of justice: God enables mankind, through the Man Jesus, to return to him of its own accord, to offer freely the love it once refused to give.

Looked at in this light, the whole process of Christ's life has a deeper significance. Everything is *not* complete at Jesus' conception — but this is not because God still clamors for his justice to be respected, but because he himself respects mankind. God wants his Christ, this Man for all men, to express in his life and death a perfect and "satisfactory" love for himself. This is atonement.

The whole of Christ's human existence is a unity. He fully identified himself with mankind's condition so that even in suffering and death he could express love. Divine love? Yes, but also a perfect human love of God. In fact, what we must try to see is that God is manifested to us *through* the perfect human love of Christ. If we set aside the human love of Christ — and this sometimes happens even in devotion to the Sacred Heart,

---

[7] In the Bible, what is called God's "justice" is much more gift-giving than condemnatory. It expresses God's will to save, his merciful fidelity to his promise of *salvation*.

whose whole purpose is to put before us Christ's human love for us — if we set aside the human love of Christ as being of little consequence compared with his divine love we have missed the point of the incarnation altogether. The human love of Christ is the only way of knowing and experiencing God's love. For God's love is expressed only in and through Christ's sacrificial love for us.

Looking at Christ historically

The lesson to be learned from all this is that Christ must be looked at not merely metaphysically but also *historically*. If today we have returned to a "history of salvation" approach in religious education, it is imperative that we restore to Christ's own life its proper historical dimensions. Rahner has written:

> Through the incarnation the whole of redemption was already preformed, even if it still had to be carried out in the suffering of death, precisely because the Logos had assumed the "flesh of sin," as St. Paul says in Rom. 8:3, in other words the flesh that is marked out for death, and a true human life that must be personally lived through, not merely a static "nature" that endures without a history. For the Logos redeemed by really identifying himself with the sinner.[8]

If we look at Christ simply in abstract fashion as divine and human, the divine in him will obscure or even swallow up the human. We must, therefore, consider Christ as a Man among men, appearing at a particular point of time that was long prepared for; he emptied himself into the condition of men which sin had brought about; he chose freely and lovingly things at variance with divinity all along the line, weakness, pain, the condition of a servant, mortality, even a shameful death upon the cross. The mystery of the incarnation is that God is revealed best precisely in those moments of Christ's life when he chooses things

---

[8] *Inquiries* (New York: Herder & Herder, 1965), p. 196.

apparently antithetical to divinity — weakness rather than strength, failure rather than success, ignominy rather than glory. God not only exists in a Man but in a Man embroiled in the sinful condition of a fallen race. All this remains hidden from those who are content to repeat "Jesus is God" and are unwilling to penetrate further into the historical process or becoming of the incarnation.

A French Catholic has expressed, in a general way, the two approaches like this: "The Catholic's vision is, as it were, perpendicular; he seeks to grasp Christ 'in himself,' and his language will always be modeled as closely as possible on the balance achieved at Chalcedon.[9] The vision and language of the Protestants follow the movement of the inspired text and usually give the impression of a Saviour on the move along the road to redemption."[10]

Most generalities of their nature tend to be imprecise, but there is much truth in these remarks. It was because Catholics — in the West more than in the East — thought and spoke of the incarnation too restrictedly in the terminology of Chalcedon that the dynamic, historical quality of Christ's life was lost. Focusing attention on the divinity of Christ, we lost sight of the paschal (or passover) mystery of Christ which is the summit of our faith and the starting point of an understanding of all the other mysteries of our faith.

In the light of what we have so far said we can express the passover of Jesus in these simple terms: The Son who came, at birth, into the world, passes over by death from this fallen world to his Father. The Father raises him from death by the power of the Spirit and establishes him as Lord, Christ, and Savior. Here is the whole movement of our redemption. The sad thing is that an exclusive concentration on Christ's divinity has made the incarnation, which is a mystery of movement, of a passage from life to death, into something static. This, in turn, explains why, among the faithful, Christmas has a more powerful attraction

---

[9] The Council of Chalcedon in A.D. 451 stated that Christ, the only begotten Son, was one person in two natures.

[10] Maurice Villain, *Unity, History and Some Reflections* (London: Harvard Press, 1963), p. 53.

than Easter: theology has not been scriptural and forcible enough
for the feast of the resurrection to challenge or vie with the
warm, human associations engendered by the feast of the nativity.
The presentation of the faith became in consequence notional
rather than, in the literal sense of the word, "event-ful," abstract
rather than functional.

In our time, the Church's renewal of the Easter Vigil (the
mother of all vigils) and the somewhat belated return of theology
to an appreciation of the passover theme, has made these matters
clearer to us than to our immediate predecessors. But it takes
some time for the points of theological reflection to be equitably
distributed among the masses.

It is only when the passover of Jesus is clearly recognized as
the central article of our faith that we are in a position to appreciate the Church's sacraments. For in the sacraments, the
ever-living Christ, the Lord of history, draws us and our whole
historically unfolding existence into his own passage through
death to life. Christianity, in this way, is seen to be more than
an assent to doctrines: it is discipleship. The pupil can sit at his
teacher's feet; the disciple must follow in his Master's footsteps,
though they lead him to a hill named after a skull.

(ii)   *The profession, "Jesus is God," is used to evacuate areas
of Christ's humanity*

So far we have concentrated on Christ's identification with
man in his sinful condition. It was a condition of debasement,
humiliation, not glorious but, on the contrary, devastating in the
loneliness it brought him, being cut off as he was in some sense
from his Father and his fellow men.

But how much was Jesus affected in his inmost being? How
much, if we may so express it, did his human condition enter
into him? We have already quoted Father Durrwell's words about

those elements within Christ into which God's glorifying holiness did not enter. He stresses that he is referring not only to Christ's body, but to all the faculties which brought him into contact with us as well. Durrwell's point of view is that of the biblical scholar, and its proponents are growing in number. It is fair comment to say that dogmatic theologians have usually been inclined to minimize, as far as possible, the effects upon Christ himself of living and moving in a sinful world. The danger is that by the time they have set down everything they consider to be entailed by Christ's divinity his humanity may almost dissolve in a blaze of glory.

The question to be resolved is: how far has Christ's divinity been used to evacuate or to negate whole areas of Christ's humanity? Here I shall be content to outline the sort of answer a theologian of today might be expected to give.

Christ is truly man

It will be objected that nothing could be clearer to the Christian mind than Christ's humanity. Was he not born, did he not grow up, become hungry and thirsty, eat, drink, and die?

But these are not, by any stretch of the imagination, what is most important to being a man. In regard to Jesus, the important question is not, Did he die, but Did he die as other men die? Or are we even going to dehumanize the dying of Jesus? dredge away all the darkness surrounding it? Are we going so to beatify Christ in his life on earth that we begin to wonder how he could have died at all? Certainly, we are less inclined to attribute any very fierce agony of mind to him when we are told that his soul looked with ecstatic happiness upon the face of God.

This seems to me to be of some interest. When asked, Is it clear that Jesus is a man? we tend to reply, Of course. He was born, hungered, thirsted, grew tired and died. Is this evidence of a somewhat naïve and superficial anthropology? To the query, Was Jesus really human? we reply by listing the things he has in common with animals. The *specifically* human, I am suggesting, we tend to annul in favor of the angelic.

To know how human Christ is, we must first set down in a summary way at least what it is to be a man. It is, evidently, to be born and to grow up loved or unloved; to distinguish oneself (one's Ego) from the surrounding world; to be taught language and to imbibe attitudes; to come to an awareness of oneself and of one's task and mission in life, and to be free to fulfil it; to struggle to fulfil one's mission, for struggle is the concomitant of freedom; to commit oneself to God in the struggle and the dark. This is not to be taken as an exhaustive list of the specifically human aspects of man's life, nor is it being suggested that these aspects are separable from the rest. I am merely pointing to an obvious fact: if we are to take as genuine the Church's profession that Jesus is truly man, the aspects just outlined must also be taken into consideration. What I am asking is: in the customary treatises on the incarnation are not some of them, at least, dismissed arbitrarily or left entirely out of consideration? When this happens, what becomes of the seriousness of the biblical and doctrinal affirmation of the complete humanity of Christ?

The approach of theological manuals

Let us look at the usual treatment of the incarnation in earlier theological manuals. *Jesus Christus est verus Deus, secunda Trinitatis Persona.* This is the first thesis in a textbook I have taken down from my shelf completely at random. "Jesus Christ is true God, the second person of the Trinity." Such a beginning establishes the sort of book we are dealing with. This is no work on the Bible, no exegetical study. It is meant to be an orderly, formal, and abstract presentation of the Christian message, and it will make its laboring, patient academic way by means of logical deductions. While we may lament that so many of our "catechisms" followed this academic, rather than the biblical approach, speculative theology, as a science, is not invalidated on that account. The first thesis enunciated above is certainly of faith. No less correct is the second thesis: "The Son of God assumed a true and integral human nature."[11] (Despite the undeniable character of these two affirmations, the danger of setting out the basic reality of Christ in two statements separated from each other by perhaps several feet of scriptural and conciliar texts ought not to escape us. The incarnation is nothing if not a mystery of unity. To this matter we will return later.)

Jesus, the one Son of God, being divine and human possessed a divine mind and a divine will as well as a human mind and a human will. These truths were thrashed out in the earliest controversies of the Church.

The attribution of the beatific vision to Christ

Now come the inferences. Jesus is God's Son, therefore. . . . Therefore, according to most theologians of an earlier period, Jesus had the beatific vision of God in his earthly life. What does the beatific vision do? It beatifies. It makes him who has it, in theological language, a *comprehensor*, one who has already attained to God. His is the fulness of spiritual happiness. His mind and heart are absorbed so ecstatically in the sight of God that no possibility of choice or sin remains. Every free choice of

---

[11] One cannot help being a little amused at the pedantry of a theologian who can qualify the thesis, "The hypostatic union is a mystery in the strict sense," as "common doctrine"! He has not been able to find a stronger note in the Councils of the Church. The reason is obvious: it was too evident to mention.

good or ill must have a motive, that is, it must have an "object" which at least appears to have a desirable quality about it. If a man's soul is confronted with God the quintessential Good, what more could he desire? To what else could he turn to look for joy and fulfilment when already he gazes face to face upon the origin and plenitude of all joy?

This, it has been affirmed, was Christ's terrestrial condition. He was God's Son, he must have had the beatific vision. When was this vision granted him? According to this textbook before me, "from the beginning." It is quite common to say that Jesus enjoyed the beatific vision from the first moment of his conception in his mother's womb. He was God's Son; *therefore* it had to be so. Matthias Scheeben, one of the best theologians of the nineteenth century, expressed in this way the common teaching of his time:

> He was the Son of God by nature. . . . Therefore His soul's participation in the divine nature meant not merely holiness and grace; it meant fully achieved glory and beatitude from the very first instant. Not only could this be so, it had to be so, unconditionally. It is unthinkable that the Son of God would not from the beginning have stood in closest and highest union with His Father even in His human nature, and that He would have strengthened and perfected this union only by degrees. But such would be the case if He had not from the first instant looked upon His Father face to face, if He had had to stand afar off like a stranger, and if, as a result, He had not been able to embrace His Father with that love in which the blessed in heaven are consumed. As there is no closer union with God than hypostatic, personal union, there can be no kind of union with God by knowledge and love that did not exist from the beginning in consequence of the hypostatic union of Christ's humanity with the Son of God. Owing to the hypostatic union, that humanity from the moment of its conception was present in God's bosom, to which creatures are raised only gradually and imperfectly; and in God's bosom it had also to gaze upon God's countenance, and to embrace God not with a love of longing and striving, but with a love of possession and fruition. Hence, as far as union with God is concerned, there was no *status viae* for Christ's humanity, as there is for us. From the very beginning Christ stood at the end of the road, at the summit of the mountain, which we must strive to gain by degrees, and to which we have

to be raised by the grace of God. Christ is a *comprehensor,* as the theologians say. He is not only holy, but also in possession of divine glory and happiness; He is transfigured and beatified.[12]

In this extract, it is said that Christ's humanity had "to embrace God not with a love of longing and striving, but with a love of possession and fruition." Why, then, today's biblical theologian will ask, does Jesus, as the end draws near, keep talking about going to the Father (e.g., Jn 14:28, 16:10, etc.)? Why does he say, with such apparent longing, to his Father, "I am coming to thee" (Jn 17:11, 13)? Scheeben claims that Christ, from the very beginning, stood "at the end of the road, at the summit of the mountain." Is this not equivalent to saying that for Christ — unlike for us — there was no road to be trod, no mountain to be climbed? What becomes of the allegedly perfect *human* quality of Christ's life as a consequence? How does such a conception fit in with the whole of John's emphasis on the primacy of the passover when for the first time Christ is glorified with the glory he had with the Father before the world began? Scheeben also claims that Christ is transfigured and glorified from the very first instant. Is it not a very peculiar form of transfiguration when the one transformed is to be the Servant of Yahweh in whom there is no comeliness and who is at length to cry out in an agony of dereliction upon a cross? Would an apostle who had witnessed the passion of Christ have recognized the Lord he loved in the speculations of Matthias Scheeben? It is doubtful if he would have been as adept as the scholastics in dividing "the human soul of Christ into different regions in order to house contradictory spiritual experiences"[13] — namely, the simultaneous fruition of, and sense of abandonment by, God. St. Thomas Aquinas himself, in order to explain this, is forced to say: "By God's powerful decree the joy of divine contemplation was kept in Christ's mind so as not to overflow into his

---

[12] *The Mysteries of Christianity* (St. Louis: B. Herder, 1951), pp. 325–326.

[13] Engelbert Gutwenger, S.J., "The Problem of Christ's Knowledge," in *Who Was Jesus Christ?* (*Concilium*) (Glen Rock, N. J.: The Paulist Press, 1966), p. 48.

powers of sense and thereby make it impossible for him to feel sensible pain."[14]

When scholastics affirmed that Christ, being God's Son, had to have a perfect humanity, did they not seem to have a very abstract notion of what perfection consists in? I do not mean to be ironical when I say that the mediaevals whom Scheeben followed in this meant by "perfect humanity" the humanity which they would have given Christ if they had been God and which (they presumed) God, being no less wise than they, had himself to give to Christ. Let us instance Christ's "perfect" knowledge. It was maintained that in the beatific vision Christ had, even during his lifetime, an actual and unlimited knowledge of everything proceeding from God; he knew the past, present, and future in its entirety. Having the function of redeemer and judge to fulfil he had to know especially all the actions of men throughout history, even their most secret thoughts.

It is interesting to see theologians who hold such a view grappling with some of the passages in scripture which are seemingly at variance with it. For example, in Mark's gospel, Christ referring to the coming of the Son of man in glory says: "Of that day or that hour no one knows, not even the angels in heaven, nor the Son, but only the Father" (13:32).

This verse is somewhat embarrassing for the theologian who argues that since Christ had the beatific vision and was the redeemer and judge of all mankind he must have known the day of the coming of the Son of man — his overt declaration of the opposite notwithstanding.

St. Thomas Aquinas took this line: the Son declares he does not know this day because he does not wish to tell it to us. He doesn't want to yield up his secret so he says: "I do not know." But he does really. The Father reveals it to the Word eternally, and the Spirit who hands on the gifts of grace reveals it to the Son as man. The Son, after all, knows every good and evil action of those taking part in the Last Judgment so *a fortiori* he must have known what was of far less importance to know: the date

---

[14] *Sum. Theol.*, 3 q. 15 a. 6 *in corp.*

of the Judgment. Christ's claim not to know it is willed nescience not true ignorance.[15]

Cardinal Cajetan, the great commentator on the works of Aquinas, thought that St. Thomas' solution of this difficult passage was inadequate. His own solution, however, seems hardly more credible. According to Cajetan, when Christ states he does not know the day of Judgment he means: "I do not know without revelation but, of course, I do know by revelation."

Both Aquinas and Cajetan are agreed on this: the one thing Christ could not have meant when he said "I do not know" is "I do not know." More recent writers interpret Mark 13:32 rather differently, as we shall see.

The infused knowledge of Christ

Apart from the beatific vision, it was once customary in theology to claim that Jesus had "infused knowledge." For the mediaevals, infused knowledge was the kind of knowledge proper to the angels. Their argument always proceeds on the supposition that Christ's knowing had to be "perfect" according to some criterion of perfection which they assumed to be evident. "It was fitting," wrote Aquinas, "that the human nature assumed by the Word of God should not be imperfect."[16] If, in the beatific vision, Jesus saw everything "in God," by means of his infused knowledge he saw things "in themselves." In each case, the knowledge was comprehensive; it extended to every sort and area of human knowledge.

We are forced to submit that the reality of Christ's manhood is looking decidedly thin. The beatific vision has set Christ among the blessed in heaven, while infused knowledge has put him in the company of the angelic hosts.

---

[15] Cf. Dom Aelred Graham in *The Christ of Catholicism* (London, 1947). "As touching a point which the Father had not charged him to reveal, he could even profess his ignorance. But deep within his mind there was no absence of knowledge of the past, present, or future" (p. 195).

[16] *Sum. Theol.*, 3, q. 9 a. 3, *in corp.*

The experimental knowledge of Christ

Feeling no doubt the pull of these objections, the scholastics hastened to affirm that there was also in Christ an acquired and experimental knowledge. There was in Jesus at least a progression of some sort of knowledge. Even here, St. Thomas is not content to think of Christ learning as other men learn. At the beginning of his teaching career Aquinas maintained that Christ's knowledge of the world was gained not from the world but directly from God. Later he humbly modified this view. Even so he claimed that while Christ's experience of the world may have been limited, from the things he did experience he was able to come to a knowledge of everything. Aquinas will not even allow that Christ, being the head of the Church, learned anything from anybody![17] It seems gratuitous, to say the least, to assert that Jesus was not dependent on his mother or St. Joseph in any way at all for what he came to understand. If Christ appeared to learn from others, presumably this was to teach us humility.

It has become increasingly difficult in recent years to accept such views about Christ. We cannot believe that Christ did not learn from men, but only seemed to be learning, or that he was not really tempted, but only gave us an example of how we ourselves should behave when faced with temptation. (A humorist might add that if Christ was not truly tempted, it is difficult to say precisely what he is giving us an example of unless it is of pretending to be tempted when one really isn't.)

What is the most vivid *impression* we take away from reading the scholastic treatment of the incarnation which has persisted right down to our own day? That Jesus is really God going through the motions of being a man when, in truth, he is not; that he is God-from-the-beyond who has put on our humanity like a space-suit. We seem to be witnessing a dehumanizing of Christ, and sometimes a dilution of the scriptures so they are made to mean the opposite of what they say. Jesus, instead of

---

[17] *Ibid.,* 3, q. 12 a. 3, *in corp.*

being one of us, a man among men, someone with whom we can identify ourselves, is supermanized, beatified, angelized. And even unlettered Catholics who know nothing about the beatific vision and who would blink uncomprehendingly were they told about Christ's "infused knowledge" are formed by people who have written or read books presupposing such views of the incarnation. Few are the teachers to whom their pupils have not said — and said repeatedly: "Imitate Jesus? How can I? It was different for him. He was God, wasn't he?" If we who are teachers groan at this, we must ask ourselves whether it is not our own non-human presentation of the mystery of the incarnation which is responsible for this misunderstanding.

In the religious formation of the young, especially of adolescents with their burning need for suitable and noble identification figures, this problem is urgent: How shall we restore, and present the features of Jesus, this Man who is one of us as well as God's only begotten and everlasting Son? It would be ludicrous to suggest that the scholastics made errors of faith about the incarnation, but was their true belief overlaid with a great deal of academic make-believe? And if so how can we retain the former while discarding the latter?

(iii)   The profession, "Jesus is God," can lead to a practical neglect of the Trinity

It is only too easy for the believer to think, "Jesus is God. It is enough if I keep him in mind always, if I always pray to him." Any informal survey made of the way Catholics pray will show that this attitude is very common. I discovered not long ago an adult's "missal" composed before the liturgical revival in which the main section was headed: "Prayers to be said at Mass." None of them had any direct references to the Church's own prayers ("said by the priest"). And they were all directed to

Jesus. Thumbing rapidly through the missal, I reached "the prayer to be said at the Our Father." Here at last, I thought, we shall have an address to the Father; but instead of the Our Father we had another prayer beginning "Dear Jesus."

It is true, naturally, that the Christian can never take his eyes off Christ. It was into him that we were all baptized. He is our life, the body of which we are the limbs, the vine of which we are the branches. Nonetheless, it does not follow from this that we should always pray *to* Jesus on the plea that he is God. In fact, the argument offered by those who pray exclusively — and they are many — to Jesus is that he is God co-equal with the Father and the Spirit. "When I pray to him," they ask, "am I not praying to the Father as well?" Certainly, the Father is honored whenever the Son is honored; and yet there is much point in reminding ourselves *to whom* we are praying. It is as important to know the answer to this as it is to know which person of the Trinity became man and died upon the cross for us. We cannot argue: Because Jesus is God and the Father is God, then the Father became man as well as the Son! Here, indeed, we are very careful about distinguishing the persons of the Trinity. We should take equal care about the distinction of the persons in our prayer. When we pray to the Father through the Son in the Spirit — and this is the most usual manner of address in the Church's own public worship — we recall the whole of God's loving plan for the human race. For it was the Father who sent his Son into the world to seek out and to save that which was lost; and it was the Son who when he was ascended to his Father sent, with him, the Spirit into our hearts so that we cry out Abba, Father (Rom 8:15–16). There is this also to be remembered: if it is true — as we shall show in the next part — that when we are "in grace" we are specially and differently related to each person of the Trinity, our prayer should be the expression in action of our supernatural condition. Living by grace, as we do, *in the Son* we are related to his Father by means of the presence in us of the Spirit who is the eternal bond of communion between Father and Son.

If we ponder these doctrines deeply we shall see the reason why the Church usually prays *through* Christ, in this way emphasizing his mediation and so his manhood. Even when we pray to the Son directly and to the Spirit as we sometimes do even in liturgical prayer we should be explicitly aware that we are praying personally to the Son and to the Spirit. The Christian, unlike the pagan, does not simply pray to God in a general way: he cannot or ought not to forget that Jesus has revealed to us the ultimate mystery of the inner life of God. God is a Trinity.

The Trinity as mystery and problem

It is sad to reflect how the word "Trinity" immediately conjures up in most Catholics' minds the notion of problem rather than mystery; and this is true even when the word "mystery" is explicitly used. It is denuded of its proper theological meaning. The Trinity is something to be puzzled over rather than to be contemplated in loving and life-giving faith. This alone can explain why, in a recent book intended as an introductory work on Catholicism for the mass-public, the author begins his chapter on the Trinity in a strangely abstract way:

> The existence of *three Persons in one Nature* is so remote from our knowledge that the triune nature of the Godhead is a Mystery of Faith. That is, reason cannot understand it although it can see there is nothing self-contradictory in the idea.[18]

It is unlikely that any Christian of any other communion could begin his exposition of the Trinity in this fashion however much he felt obliged to accept the decrees of the early councils of the Church in which the metaphysical notions of person and nature were employed. It would seem ludicrous to him to speak of the Trinity first of all as something which exercises the *mind*, as a

---

[18] David Quinlan, *Roman Catholicism* (The Teach Yourself Books) (London, 1966), p. 7.

"truth" which, if it is not to be solved, has to be reconciled with ordinary arithmetical tautologies, for example, that one is one and not three. He would automatically start his treatment in a *biblical* way by following the historical unfolding of the Trinity. In this unfolding, Christ holds the central place, for it is he who makes the Father *present* and *known*, and who sends the Spirit upon us when his mortal days on earth are ended. The Trinity is hardly to be thought of as, in the first place, an abstract puzzle: it is above all a matter of personal communing with the three divine persons who have entered unmistakably and with power into our own life history. However, if Christ the Man — who because he is a man reveals God in the time series — slips from view, then the Trinity necessarily receives the "shamrock-treatment." Instead of being revealed in historical action (the incarnation, the resurrection, pentecost) the blessed Trinity remains hidden in metaphysical abstraction.

The following words of a priest-student of mine express in a sad and synthetic way what he finds wrong with "Catholic" prayer-life.

> I have discovered since I became a Catholic that the concept, "Jesus Christ who is God," is so deep in people's minds that not only has the humanity of Jesus faded into obscurity, but God the Father has also disappeared, or at least become fused and merged with the Sacred Heart. The Trinity as revealed has become a different "trinity," with Christ our Lord taking over the Father's role, our Lady becoming the mediator, and grace — thought of more like a material entity — replacing the Spirit as the sanctifier. To speak of a Christ-centered catechesis means little if the revealed Trinity is shelved as an inexplicable mathematical puzzle and the term "Christ" reduced to the "surname" of Jesus and interchangeable with it.

When our fellow Christians accuse us Catholics of worshipping Mary, of treating her as divine, we rightly reply: Nonsense. But what probably underlies this objection is the feeling that Catholics — despite their protestations to the contrary — do put Mary in place of Christ as the mediator between God and men. If Jesus is thought of exclusively as God then the objection has some validity, for in this case Mary, instead of uniting us to

"Jesus our mediator," unites us to "Jesus our God." This is equivalent to saying that Mary is the mediator between God and men.

Again, I must insist, I am not dealing with the level of credal profession but with that of behavioral response. *In practice*, do we treat our Lady in the fashion I have described? Are the criticisms of our fellow-Christians as far off the mark as we tend to assume? Is the mediation of Christ the Man so clear in our minds that we are constantly aware of our inability to approach God or have our prayers heard except we come to him "through Jesus Christ our Lord"?

The strategy of Christian prayer

When Christ's mediation is properly appreciated the Trinity becomes more than a notion on which we exercise our wits so as to preserve it from the charge of self-contradiction. We live a trinitarian life. The strategy of Christian prayer becomes evident: we pray to God our Father, through Jesus the mediator in the holy Spirit who joins us to the risen and Spirit-filled Lord. To be clear on this strategy is more important than anything else, for the first question about prayer which imposes itself upon us is not, "Am I praying with zest and perseverance?" but "Am I praying *as a Christian?*"

Christ's mediation can only preserve its centrality in our faith when his manhood is completely real to us. This is probably the prime task of theology today: to convince the faithful that God's Son is truly a man among men and not God in fancy dress. One way to achieve this is to refer to Christ not simply as God — the term usually applied to the Father in the New Testament — but as the Son (or God's Son). If this simple rule of language is kept — usually even if not always — it will make an extraordinary difference to our faith and prayer. For the Son is only Son by reference to the Father whom he manifests and whose name we can utter only because the Spirit has been sent into our hearts. After a while — it may be a long while if we were not brought up on a trinitarian devotion — we will automatically think of the Father when "God" is mentioned, and approach him through his beloved Son whose prayer is always heard for his reverence (Heb 5:7) and in the power of the indwelling Spirit.

SEEING THE FACE OF CHRIST

It may be objected that the express treatment of the incarnation so far has been too negative. Something very positive was intended: that the face and figure of a Man should emerge. This picture is at once unfamiliar and familiar, unfamiliar to the readers of earlier manuals and catechisms, but strangely familiar to those who pore over the source book of revelation, the scriptures. In fact, the major aim of my approach has been to send the Christian teacher racing back to the Bible itself and not first of all to catechisms or textbooks where the immediacy of Christ's presence has been lost. Every page of the scriptures, Old Testament as well as New, must be scanned so as to reveal the true face of Christ on which God has shone the light of his glory.

A second objection might well take this form: we have read a great deal about Christ's manhood, when are we going to be told about his divinity?

To say that Jesus is God's incarnate Son is equivalent to saying that we cannot talk about his humanity without talking about his divinity. This would not be so if Jesus were only a man dwelt in by God, but he is not. He is the Word made flesh. Theology is the study of this man. "He who has seen me has seen the Father" (Jn 14:9). Those who may be worried by the second objection have failed to realize that there is for us no naked vision of God. We only see God as he is revealed in the life,

death, and resurrection of Jesus. If when we read the Old Testament stories of Abraham and the Exodus we are also learning
about God, how much more is it true to say that we learn about
God through the events of Christ's life. When we look at Jesus
we see God with us, God given to us. For the incarnation translates into the conditions of our world the very being of the
eternal Son who is ever one with, open to, and in love with his
Father. As the Image of God, the Son in eternity mirrors the
Father's majesty; and in time he reflects that same majesty, in
so far as this is possible, in the manhood he assumed. This is
why Jesus says categorically: "He who has seen me has seen the
Father." He does not say: "When a man sees me it will be as *if*
he has seen the Father."

The way of approach to the mystery of the incarnation has,
it is to be hoped, been illumined by these reflections. We must
not read the divine *into* Christ's human life, we must read the
divine *off* his human life. The Latin textbook to which I referred
earlier by beginning with a *truth* (the divinity of Christ) instead
of a human life reverses the correct order of investigation. This
procedure serves to explain why manuals are not interested in
the ordinary events of Christ's life from a theological standpoint:
the parables, debates, disputes, and the "ordinary" incidents are
left to the exegete to deal with, as if they have no revelatory
significance, as if they tell us nothing about divinity.

It is not right for us to keep repeating "Jesus is divine," as if
we know what divinity is all about, as if our knowledge of it
were so comprehensive that we can even argue a *priori* what
must have been entailed by it for Christ's humanity. Let us not
assume that the doctrine "Jesus is divine" is crystal clear to us,
anterior to and independent of the events of this Man's life.
God is and always will be the unknowable who reveals himself
in the life-history of Jesus of Nazareth. That life-history is the
very existence of God in the world, the very presence and revelation of God to mankind. Every element in it is precious as
revelatory of God, it is precious in the lowliness and frailty of
it as well as in its grandeur. Lowliness and frailty demonstrate

the authenticity of Christ's human life and so manifest God in a way no pagan could have dreamed of. God comes to master men in the weakness of Christ. Paul did not say, "God forbid I should glory save in the divinity of Christ," but "God forbid I should glory save in the cross of Christ." Still, he knew that here, above all, is "the power of God and the wisdom of God" (1 Cor 1:24).

Seeing Christ in scripture

It takes some courage to look squarely at the scriptures, to behold, without theological planks in our eyes, the man.

We see someone born of a poor village girl, and living in a despised provincial town in the north from which nothing good was expected to come. Since God's Son is truly a man, and since he was destined to express God through the human, Mary by her fashioning and guidance of Christ has a special role in revelation itself. She it was who taught Jesus how to pray in his earliest years when his human consciousness first awoke to God his Father. As Père Congar writes: "What he had learned, experienced, and understood, as a child, then as an adult, in the practice of the Jewish religion, entered, as the sketch into the completed work, into the revelation and the institution of the new covenant which he contained within himself."[19] Congar also says:

> All the filial obedience of Jesus is summed up in his passion, by which our salvation is effected. He had practiced it throughout his life and, by this very practice, he had humanly better understood and deepened it. He had been trained by his parents and he had learned it from them, just as he had learned from them, and from his teachers, and from his Jewish background, love and respect for the temple, religious and basic acts, prayer, the psalms, the primary import of passover and of the feasts which,

---

[19] *Jesus Christ* (New York: Herder & Herder, 1966), p. 63.

by the witness of St. John, he was to make the context of so much teaching, of so many messianic acts.

In this way, the human feelings, the dispositions of heart and of will, by means of which Jesus effected our salvation, had gradually been formed in his experience as a young Jew, and in his education at Nazareth by Mary and Joseph.[20]

The incident of Jesus' loss in the temple at passover time when he was twelve is certainly mysterious. Luke's intention, however, is clearly to show Christ's humanity and possibly his thrill at being in the temple of his Father and able to ask learned men about the scriptures which he himself pondered at such depth. It is in his hidden years that Jesus' understanding of his mission was being formed.

Afterwards, Jesus returned to Nazareth with his parents. Franz Michael Willam wrote: "Champions of 'Evolution' claim to have established a process of evolution in Jesus' consciousness of his divine sonship. However, so far as concerns his real self-consciousness, and not a pedagogical development of theological truths, there is no trace of development between his first recorded words: 'Did you not know that I must be about my Father's business?' and the last words of the crucified Miracle-Worker: 'Father, into thy hands I commend my spirit.' "[21] These sentiments seem a very strange comment on a story which ends with: "And Jesus increased in wisdom and in stature, and in favour with God and man" (Lk 2:52). But more will be said of Jesus' consciousness later.

When Jesus began his ministry so vividly depicted in Mark's gospel, the earliest account we have, he showed himself to be capable of surprised wonder and a mighty anger and tears. No doubt, he had to learn, as all teachers do, how difficult it was to "get through" to his disciples. He claimed not to know certain things. He often tried to get away from the crowds to find a bit of peace, to be in the quieter, more relaxed atmosphere and society of friends.

Here was a man who, because he was a man, was in need of

---

[20] *Ibid.*, pp. 54–55.
[21] *The Life of Jesus Christ* (St. Louis: B. Herder, 1936), p. 57.

men. He needed them to love him, and himself needed to love them. Unless he loved them he could not have come to his own full stature as a man; he could not have fulfilled himself. He was truly a brother among brothers.

He found parts of his life a trial and a burden, and as his days wore on he yearned deeply for happier times. He wanted keenly to be glorified, to be with his Father. His relation to his Father is the key to everything. Christ could be the perfect servant of his fellows because he was really humble before God, accepting God's will gratefully. It is because as man he accepted everything from God as a gift that he did not "lord it over others" but served them with a total dedication. It is possible to teach and preach the incarnation, and, if not to leave Christ's relationship to his Father out of account altogether, at least to see it only inconstantly and on rare occasions. Yet, for Jesus, this relationship to his Father was the joy and moving passion of his life. He had come into the world only to do his Father's will, and he always did the things that pleased him. Jesus lived in, for and out of that relationship of love and obedience to his Father. He is literally constituted by that relationship: he is "the Son."

But he is the Son who has "come." He is a man and so he needs to pray — he needs to pray, not to give us an example of prayer, but out of terrible need. He goes off into mountains to converse with his Father all the night. He prays most when the need is heaviest upon him, in the agony of Gethsemane when he goes apart to meet his Father and tastes the sheer terror of approaching death.

He knew, too, the sweetness of answered prayer. He was confident that his prayer was always heard, and this is why he tells his followers that their prayer in his name can never fail. It becomes one with his own filial prayer to the Father in whom he wholly trusted. Yes, he trusted in his Father even in the darkness, even when he experienced in utter abandonment the hell of death. "At the ninth hour Jesus cried with a loud voice, 'Eloi, Eloi, lama sabach-thani?' which means, 'My God, my God, why hast thou forsaken me?'" (Mk 15:34.) Jesus prayed Psalm 22 because it was written of him, because he was "a worm, and no man; scorned by men and despised by the people" (Ps 22:6). He could equally as well have quoted the lament of Job in his dereliction:

> If I speak, my pain is not assuaged . . .
> Surely now God has worn me out;
>   he has made desolate all my company.
> And he has shrivelled me up . . .
> God gives me up to the ungodly,
>   and casts me into the hands of the wicked . . .
> He set me up as his target,
>   his archers surround me . . .
> My face is red with weeping,
>   and on my eyelids is deep darkness;
> although there is no violence in my hands,
>   and my prayer is pure.
> O earth, cover not my blood,
>   and let my cry find no resting place.
> Even now, behold, my witness is in heaven,
>   and he that vouches for me is on high.
>   (Job 16:6–19.)

On the cross he kept saying — and it was hard, for he was a man and no man was more sensitive to injustice than he — he kept saying: "Father forgive them; they know not what they do" (Lk 23:34). "Forgive Herod (that 'Fox'); and Pilate who declared me guiltless before condemning me to death; and Judas who screamed in remorse, 'I have betrayed the blood of an innocent man.' Forgive all like them."

God's Son is a man

What emerges from this examination of ours? That Jesus' humanity was no puppet whose strings were pulled by a divine person (the Word). When we deny that Jesus is a "human person" isn't this the sort of picture that sometimes comes before our minds?

It is true that ultimately everything Jesus did and said and had done to him is attributable to the Word of God, but he is no marionette of a man. He is fully, consciously, autonomously a man. If he is not, then the Son did not become man at all but only assumed a human form. The Council of Chalcedon decreed that Jesus is a divine person in a human and divine nature. By the terms "one person, two natures" the Council wanted to say something positive. It is not sufficient to repeat "Jesus is not a human person." Rather, we must stress positively the fact that the Son of God is a man. This we could not do if there were two persons in Christ. We would not be able, for example, to say in this case, "The Son died on the cross," but only, "Jesus of Nazareth who is distinct from God's Son died upon the cross."

Chalcedon's positive declaration has been nullified; its affirmation of the uniqueness of person in Christ has been utilized, as we saw earlier, to minimize Christ's humanity. It is very necessary in teaching adolescents to show that the Church's belief in Jesus as the one Son of God, a single divine person, is paradoxically the doctrine which safeguards *the humanity of God's Son.* He is truly, autonomously a man. God's Son is very man, someone who wept, and loved, was betrayed and crucified. These things are not attributed to him as if they were outside him. God's Son has taken the human condition completely to himself.

The consciousness of Christ

Since there is so much speculation at present about the consciousness of Christ it is worth mentioning briefly this most difficult subject, if only in a tentative and exploratory way. It will also provide an opportunity for giving the views of some contemporary theologians on the scope and character of Christ's knowledge which are in marked contrast with those of the scholastics.

First, let us remember that Christ's human mind, being finite, could not exhaustively fathom his own divinity. The obviousness of this statement has the value of reminding us that just because Jesus is divine, his human mind does not cease to be creaturely, and so, limited. What can be said of the workings of this human mind?

Jesus, being authentically human, was "present to himself" as all men are. This is what it means to be self-conscious, or aware of oneself. Self-consciousness accompanies the knowledge of anything we say or do: we are aware that *I* am saying this, *I* am doing this. Christ also had this reference-center for all his thoughts and actions, a psychological Ego we might call it. In fact, it is necessary to speak of the human personality of Christ.[22] Christ as man is aware of the uniqueness of himself as this man with this particular life-history which belongs personally to the Word.

Jesus presumably came to self-awareness, in the sense I have explained, in the course of time. Self-awareness (the capacity for reflective thought) depends upon the development of the brain.[23] If the brain is not sufficiently developed, or if it is damaged, no thinking or self-consciousness is possible. So it was with Jesus. He came, as time went on, to be aware of himself as thinking, choosing, acting. But he was also simultaneously and immediately aware that he was God's Son in this absolutely unique manner. He didn't argue to any of this. These are not things which it is possible to argue to. He was aware — and all his speech testifies to this — that his whole human being was dedicated, and given over to the Word and existed by the Word. In short, he was aware that he, Jesus of Nazareth, was God's Son. When some scribes, hearing him forgive sins, complain, "It is blasphemy! Who can forgive sins but God alone?" Jesus turns to the paralytic

---

[22] Cf. Hans Urs von Balthasar, *A Theology of History*, pp. 10, 22.

[23] Scholastics say that thought is "extrinsically" dependent on the brain. They mean by this that the brain, being a material organ, is not the same as intelligence, a spiritual power. A man does not think *with* his brain. But because man is both bodily and spiritual, he cannot think if he is *without* a brain. Just because a man cannot think when his brain is injured, it does not follow that when his brain is uninjured he thinks with *that*. At least, this is the scholastics' contention.

and tells him to rise, take up his pallet and go home, "that you may know that the Son of man has authority on earth to forgive sins" (Mk 2:7, 10). While Jesus' human mind could not comprehend his own divinity, without a doubt he experienced divine Sonship in his human consciousness. This direct awareness of his is beyond all our capacity to grasp or fathom. It is what Karl Adam calls "his theandric consciousness of identity" with the Word. It might be suggested further, however, that Jesus, being a man, was able to reflect on his own divine Sonship, to discover more fully what it meant to be the Son of God made man, and express and re-express his Sonship to himself by means of *ideas* available to him in his historical situation. Something analogous happens in our own human thinking: we know immediately and always *that* we exist without having to prove it or argue to it, whereas *what* we are (spiritual beings, immortal, etc.) requires investigation, hard thinking and the utilization of complex ideas. Or we might find an analogy in this: we know, in one sense, who we are as soon as we awake to consciousness but this grasp of who we are becomes more developed as our life unfolds in space-time and through personal encounters with others.

As to the character and scope of Christ's knowledge, theologians today are less "generous" in their estimate of its perfection. No vision of God can be attributed to Christ which would make genuine, bitter pain impossible to him and any increase in knowledge superfluous. They are unwilling to consider Jesus as being able to see all things past, present, and future from his conception or in early childhood when he was as yet unable to distinguish himself psychologically from surrounding colors and objects. They react strongly against the picture given in some devotional works of Jesus meditating as a boy upon his passion and crucifixion! Christ was not a *comprehensor*, as Scheeben supposed.

Rahner argues that freedom of choice is only possible where there is a certain area of the unknown ahead into which freedom plunges us. Had Christ known the future in exact detail he, too, would have been without freedom of choice. Such knowledge would have pointed out to him the way to be trodden without

him having (or even being able) to resolve the crisis for himself.
It is, after all, classical in scholasticism that freedom of choice is
liberum arbitrium, free judgment. If foresight shows that the
judgment is "already taken," as it were, then the individual can
follow that judgment, he cannot make it himself as if his choice
constituted an entirely new beginning. Knowledge of the future
is, in this respect, quite different from knowledge of the possibilities of the future even if these possibilities are exhaustively
known. Knowledge of possibilities leaves a man's judgment about
what is to be done unimpaired. Knowledge of the real future
would entail that the judgment has already been taken, the crisis
has already been resolved. That which is essential to true freedom,
the personal resolution of a crisis, has thereby been removed.
Christ's life is not authentically human if he is not called upon
to decide for himself what is to be done, what it is that God
wills him to do in the various changing circumstances of his life.

We might instance Christ's temptation in the desert. This was
for him a completely new situation, the crisis of which he resolved by means of prayer and meditation on his people's history
of trials in the desert. Since Christ was truly free, he possessed
an authentic freedom of judgment. Here he was called upon to
approach this fresh trial and *see* it as God meant him to see it,
to *judge* it as his Father wished him to. We tend to think that
Jesus knew in advance what was demanded of him and then
simply had to act in accord with what he knew. This perhaps
explains why not only we but many of the fathers of the Church
like St. Leo find it hard to understand how Christ had anything
to contend with. We even ask: "Could Jesus really be tempted?"
We would more readily answer in the affirmative if we realized
that the initial struggle of Christ was in knowing what God
wanted him to do, in *coming to see* situations from God's point
of view and accepting that viewpoint. This struggle to see — a
genuine struggle — is the exercise of freedom, for Jesus did not
shirk from looking at things in the way his Father wanted.

In the desert, revelation continues to take place in Christ's
human consciousness. From his earliest years in Nazareth until

his death the Father's will is gradually and, in the event, painfully made manifest to him. Christ, then, is the *recipient* of revelation and his reception is conditioned by his ever-changing human situation. In the brief scriptural phrase, "he was tempted," we are made aware that Jesus was facing a new encounter with God and a new encounter with forces opposed to God. Caught in the midst of the conflict of such terrible encounters he emerges triumphant, resolved to do his Father's will although it meant lowliness and ignominy and failure in the world's eyes.

Contemporary theology

To show how different is the approach of some contemporary theologians to that of St. Thomas Aquinas it is best to quote one or two passages in full. In this way, the reader will be able to judge for himself how much of a change has occurred or is occurring in the presentation of the incarnation.

Karl Adam in his lectures delivered over a number of years at Tübingen — they were published in English in 1957 under the title *The Christ of Faith* — was already exploring in depth the intellectual perfection of Christ's humanity. He writes of the progression in Jesus' natural knowledge of himself:

> When the Epistle to the Hebrews assures us that Jesus learned obedience from the things that he suffered, it indicates that he came to understand the sorrowful experiences that he was increasingly compelled to make in proclaiming his tidings, with a more profound and vivid awareness of their mysterious connection with his Father's will. The Evangelists are one in their account that on the day of Caesarea Philippi, when Peter first avowed him to be the Christ, he "began" also to speak of his suffering. Now it is certain that from the beginning ever since his human consciousness first awoke and he felt himself to be the well-beloved Son of the heavenly Father, Jesus also knew in advance that his calling was one of suffering. For it was written in the prophets that the Son of Man must suffer in order to enter into his glory. But at the beginning it would seem that

this suffering loomed before his soul obscurely, imprecisely, as an inevitable destiny. At first he did not know its details; he had no idea of when his suffering would begin, nor the particularly terrible form his execution would take. Only when he arose to make his pilgrimage to Jerusalem, the centre of orthodox Jewry, only as opposition to his message increased, and hostile groups were formed against him, and attempts on his life were made, only then did his natural understanding attain the knowledge through experience (*scientia experimentalis*) that his death for our salvation was near. So Jesus learned the details of his passion only by way of his advancing personal experience in immediate contact with his situation, which daily grew more critical.[24]

Adam, following John the Evangelist very carefully, claims that Christ had a supernatural mode of knowing, a direct vision of the divine essence. "When the triune God endowed him with the incarnation, he also gave him the knowledge of this incarnation as soon as his human consciousness was sufficiently mature to understand the union."[25]

While Jesus had a direct intuitive vision of the Word and so of the divine nature, Adam follows the great mediaeval theologian Scotus in putting limits to this vision. For Adam, Jesus' human soul is not actually but only potentially confronted with the abundance and totality of the vision of God. He thinks that without some limitation, freedom and suffering would have been impossible for Christ. Hence he speaks of Christ's "relative omniscience." He writes: "It is omniscient because in principle it comprehends everything that God knows. And it is a relative omniscience because it is given only potentially, only according to its capabilities, and put into action only successively, from one case to the next, according to the decision of Jesus' free will."[26] When Christ claims not to know the day of Judgment, according to Adam, he means it to be taken literally. "Because Jesus' human soul belonged to the self of the Logos, all knowledge is objectively and in principle available to it. His possession of it was potential."[27] But he did not always draw upon this knowledge as in this instance.

[24] *The Christ of Faith* (New York: Mentor Omega, 1964), p. 263.
[25] *Ibid.*, p. 267.   [26] *Ibid.*, p. 270.   [27] *Ibid.*, p. 275.

Piet Schoonenberg, S.J. writes in the same vein though, on this rare occasion, with less theological subtlety. What follows is very reminiscent of the longest passage of Karl Adam quoted above:

> For Jesus, the "choice of his career" is that he does not continue the job of a carpenter in Nazareth but — suddenly or gradually — decides to lead the life of a preacher. By doing this he joins the existing career of the peripatetic rabbi. Within this framework Jesus makes a fresh choice and the most important one of his life: instead of political leadership he choses the function of a defenseless prophet. In all this it is probable that Jesus became only gradually clear about the circumstances of his life and the direction his life should take. At his baptism Jesus may not have seen yet that the painful end of the Servant of Yahweh would be his. Perhaps the fact that Jesus let himself be baptized by John shows that until then he considered himself a disciple of the baptizing prophet rather than a prophet in his own right. What happened immediately after his baptism must not be understood as an epiphany of the Christ to the crowd but rather as a theophany or divine experience for Jesus himself; as such it implies that, from that moment, he recognized in himself the figure of the Servant of Yahweh. Does he already foresee then that his death will have the significance of that vicarious sacrifice of atonement, described in Isaiah 53? Against this it must be said that at the start of his preaching Jesus links the coming of God's kingdom only with the conversion of his hearers; that he only begins to foretell his passion after the hardening of the attitude of the Jewish leaders, and then only within the circle of his disciples (see, for instance, Mt 16). Only when the opposition grows and these opponents develop a truly deadly hatred of him, there dawns upon him the significance of the violent death which awaits him. Now he recognizes from the circumstances that his Father's will for him is to fulfill the function of the Servant of Yahweh to the end, to die in order to bring the many to righteousness. Thus his horizon broadens out from the lost sheep of Israel to Jew and gentile, and his mission develops from that of a prophet proclaiming salvation to that of the victim bringing salvation.[28]

Englebert Gutwenger, S.J. in the same number of *Concilium*

---

[28] In *Who Was Jesus of Nazareth?*, pp. 34–35. This volume of *Concilium* probably gives the best overall picture of Christology that there is at present. It also has the advantage of being not too technical.

speaks in similar terms of a progression in Christ's understanding
of his mission:

> In his missionary work Jesus addressed himself in principle to
> Israel. Only later on did he see the failure of his mission. And
> later still did he realize that he had to suffer and die. But even
> in his early prediction of his suffering the thought of a death
> for atonement was not present yet. Here, too, there seems to
> have been a development in the understandings of his mission.[29]

Hans Urs von Balthasar, S.J. also has some interesting reflections on Christ's knowledge. In the scriptures, Christ's "hour" is
spoken of as "coming," he says. It is something that cannot be
summoned.

> Not even by knowledge (Mk 13:32), for that too would be an
> anticipation, disturbing the sheer, naked unqualified acceptance
> of what comes from the Father. . . . When the hour comes and
> the Father gives it to him as supreme fulfilment and glorification
> (Jn 12:23), as the supreme gift of his love, the Son will not
> want to say to the Father that he has always known this hour,
> that it holds nothing new for him, brings only what has been
> long familiar, what he has always savoured through and through,
> in thought, already handled and thumbed over and fingered in
> his mind. He wants rather to receive it so fresh, so immediately
> born out of the eternal source of all love, that there will be no
> trace, no fingerprint of anything on it except the Father's will.
> Of course the Son would be *"able"* to know it and take the
> measure of it beforehand — but then he would not be the Son,
> but more like some superman upon whom men have projected
> their own longings as attributes of perfection.[30]

Von Balthasar goes on to affirm that Christ's knowledge as
God-man is measured by his mission. His perfection essentially
consists of an obedience which does not anticipate, of a *patience*
which is the only model of ours. He waits, he allows himself to
be *led* like a lamb. The author continues:

> To regard Christ's knowledge as though he carried out his actions
> in time from some vantage-point of eternity — rather like a
> chess-player of genius who quickly foresees the whole course of
> the game which for him is already over — would be to do away
> entirely with his temporality and so with his obedience, his pa-

---

[29] *Ibid.*, p. 54.
[30] *A Theology of History*, p. 31.

tience, the merit of his redemptive existence; he would no longer be the model of a Christian existence and of Christian faith. He would no longer be qualified to narrate the parables of expectation and waiting which describe the life of his followers.[31]

Brother Gabriel Moran says that there should be no great problem about attributing nescience to Christ and so real human development. He writes:

> Contemporary theology's insistence upon the limitations of Christ's knowledge is not intended to denigrate his greatness as man. Christ possessed human knowledge to an extraordinary degree, but it was *human* knowledge, that is, partial, temporal, experimental. Whereas mediaeval theology thought that it was fitting to attribute all gifts and all knowledge to Christ's humanity, we realize today that it is more fitting and more accurate to see Christ living his human life as the recapitulation of man's revelational history, like to us in all things save sin. Whereas mediaeval theology made no distinction between an immediate knowledge of God and the "beatific vision," contemporary theology attributes to Christ a direct knowledge of God that is not necessarily beatifying while he is on earth.[32]

Finally, we ought to mention Karl Rahner's long essay "Christology within an Evolutionary View."[33] It is difficult but of exceptional value for understanding the new approach to the consciousness of Christ. He writes:

> . . . we wish to indicate . . . that right from the beginning one ought not to speak here of a "beatific vision." For one thing, it is far too easily taken for granted as self-evident that direct contact with God must always be beatific. . . . Furthermore, is it certain that what is meant, in the tradition of theology, by the consciousness of Christ is really intended to convey an idea of beatitude by direct union with God over and above this union? In view of the data provided by the historical sources regarding Christ's death-agony on the cross, can one seriously maintain — without applying an artificial layer psychology — that Jesus enjoyed the beatitude of the blessed, thus making of him someone who no longer really and genuinely achieves his human existence as a "viator" . . . ? When we hear about Christ's direct vision of God, we instinctively imagine this vision as a vision of the

---

[31] *Ibid.*, p. 32.
[32] *Theology of Revelation* (New York: Herder & Herder, 1966), pp. 69–70.
[33] Chapter 8 of *Theological Investigations*, Vol. 5 (Baltimore: Helicon, 1966).

divine essence present before his mind's eye as an object as if
the divine essence were an object being looked at by an observer
standing opposite it . . . then we pass equally unconsciously and
naturally to the thought that this divine essence offering itself
and viewed in this way as an object of vision from without, is
like a book or mirror offering, and putting before Christ's consciousness, more or less naturally all other conceivable contents
of knowledge in their distinct individuality. . . . But can such a
consciousness have been that of the historical Jesus as we know
him from the gospels — the consciousness of one who questions,
doubts, learns, is surprised, is deeply moved, the consciousness
of the one who is overwhelmed by a deadly feeling of being fore-
saken by God?[34]

Rahner goes on to show that Christ's "vision" of God is not
like the vision of an object. Although he already possessed God,
was basically present to God from the start, he still had the un-
ending task of grasping what and who he was in more express
and reflex terms. We must, Rahner tells us, speak without qualms
of a spiritual and religious development in Jesus. There was in
him as in us a "history of his own personal self-interpretation of
himself to himself." He gradually came, that is, to grasp better
what he always basically knew: himself. As to the things that
Christ did not know:

We would grant that this kind of initial nescience existed, but
would absolutely deny that there are declarations by the Church's
magisterium or theologically binding traditions which do not
allow us to accept such a nescience. In fact, it must be said that
if the doctrine of the true, genuine human nature of the Son
as essentially similar to our own is not to be degraded into a
myth of a god disguised in a human appearance — such a his-
toricity and "coming from beginnings" in which what was yet
to come (precisely because it was historical) was not always
already present, must necessarily be attributed to Jesus.[35]

Agreeing with Karl Adam, Rahner tells us that we must hold
to the direct vision of the Logos by Christ's soul. *Implicitly*
Christ's knowledge would extend to everything connected with
his saving mission. However, we are not "to suppose for this
reason that Jesus possessed a permanent, reflex and fully-formed

---

[34] *Ibid.*, pp. 203–207.
[35] *Ibid.*, p. 213.

propositional knowledge of everything after the manner of an encyclopaedia or of a huge, actually completed world-history."[36]

Seeing anew the personality of Christ

We see in these excerpts, the length of which I feel sure the reader will forgive, an attempt being made to present Christ as truly and fully human. We ought not to forget the tentative, probing nature of these authors' enquiries. Schoonenberg repeatedly uses the phrases, "it is probable," "perhaps," "Jesus may not have seen," etc. It would be unwise to want to be any more dogmatic than this. We ought to try to be always humble in our enquiries into the unfathomable mystery of Christ. One thing is certain: the recent approaches will strike many as being more reverent toward the mystery of the incarnation than the older custom of attributing a comprehensive knowledge of past, present, and future to the infant Christ. It may well be that Adam, Schoonenberg, Gutwenger, Von Balthasar, Rahner, and others are expressing things that we have hitherto half thought and dared not think out fully, and certainly dared not say.

Christ is shown by authors such as these to be a man among men, coming slowly as children do to self-awareness; being aware at the same time that he is God's Son in a unique sense, and yet elaborating and interpreting this truth by means of the concepts available to him. His consciousness of being God's Son still left him perhaps in the dark about God's will for him. His human mind had no exhaustive grasp of his divinity, and it would seem reasonable to suppose that he had to bide his time until his Father's will was revealed to him in its completeness.

Much of Christ's life, according to this scheme, is a groping toward the light. He willingly waited patiently upon his Father until, through the stress of events and the fluctuations of cir-

---

[36] *Ibid.*, p. 214.

cumstance, his Father showed him what he had to do. When, by reason of his brethren's rejection of him, Jesus' role as the servant of Yahweh became clearer to him, he accepted it. He did so freely. He was free to lay down his life, to give his life as a ransom for many. All the time he trusted fully in his Father; he believed that the sepulcher would not be the end but that he "would see the fruit of the travail of his soul and be satisfied" (Is 53:11).

Conclusion

If the general lines of approach in this chapter are correct something dramatic has emerged, and yet something we always confessed our faith in: the complete manhood and mediation of Christ. We must not use the divinity of Christ to evacuate whole areas of Christ's manhood, for when we do this our understanding of divinity correspondingly diminishes. We cannot know God except by looking at Jesus.

When we look at Jesus we see not a static "nature" but an emergent personality, a man like ourselves with a history, with a life to be lived through. It is in our world that he walks, a world of imperfection and godlessness. Here he came to know the loneliness and darkness of our condition of sin. Here he obeyed perfectly and flawlessly loved his Father. And when his hour came for which he had longed, he greeted the cross which was to be the means by which he terminated his life-history. This termination was a consummation, for by death he passed over from this world to his Father, was perfected (Heb 5:9) and glorified (Jn 17:5). Christ died for us "while we were yet sinners" (Rom 5:8).

Now we must proceed to examine the doctrine of original sin. Freedom from original sin is often said to be the first fruit of Christ's passion. "As one man's trespass led to condemnation for all men, so one man's act of righteousness leads to acquittal and life for all men" (Rom 5:18).

PART III

Original sin

A controversial subject

There is no subject more liable to cause teachers to tear their hair out and children to profess a belligerent unbelief than original sin. The subject cannot be avoided either, since baptism, according to most catechisms, first of all "cleanses us from original sin."

At the beginning let me admit that some of what I shall say will seem perilously like hair-splitting. Academic theology — what someone has labelled "theological infighting" — is not to everybody's taste. It could be that in a few years general agreement will have been reached on matters which at present are decidedly controversial.

For some years past many of our fellow Christians have been propounding views on original sin which our own theologians more or less unanimously decided were heretical. Gradually, however, and mostly in a tentative and exploratory fashion, some Catholic thinkers have begun to espouse at least some aspects of these modern opinions. I propose, therefore, even if only to clear the air a little, to give as accurate an account as I can of the classical view of original sin and the attacks which it has sustained of late. My aim, I would insist from the outset, is to inform and not to judge, to clarify problems and not to solve them. This section is the work of an expositor and not a critic. The most I can do is to try to give a comparatively simple outline of the most vast and probably the most complex problem in contemporary theology. The final judgment on the more recent interpretations of original sin belongs to the Church, and obviously there are limits to what is allowable. "These limits," said Pope Paul on July 11, 1966, to a select group of theologians engaged in studying the question, "are drawn by the living teaching authority of the Church, which is the supreme norm for all the faithful."

Should the Church decide vigorously against the recent attempts to recast the doctrine of original sin there will still be enough riches unearthed by theologians in the making of these attempts to merit our respect and our thanks. The permanent gains I shall try to indicate toward the end of this part.

The truth of the book of Genesis

We know that the story which we find in the early chapters of Genesis is a pictorial representation of theological truth. Few people today believe that it took God literally six days to create the world. The author did not intend us to understand his writings like that. This is easily shown. Day, for instance, is made before the sun, as are the plants, and even a simpleton knows that without the sun there can be no division of day and night nor can any plants live and grow. Moreover, those who take everything in the Bible literally — "fundamentalists" they are called — have a problem confronting them from the word

go in that the sequence of events recorded in chapter one of
Genesis differs from that of chapter two. (These two chapters
were written down in their present form by different authors,
the first at the time of the Babylonian Exile in the sixth century B.C., the second before the Exile, which means that both
appeared very late in Israel's history.)

The fundamentalist is making a mistake about the *kind* of
literature to be found at the beginning of Genesis, the sort of
mistakes made by the older editions of the scriptures when,
following Bishop Usher and Isaac Newton, they tell us that the
year of creation was 4004 B.C., or by an Evengelical who once in-
formed me that God took 6000 years to make the world because
with God "a thousand years are as a single day." Genesis is not of
a piece with *The Cambridge Modern History* nor is it a work of
mysticism. It is a story. It speaks of God creating for six days
and resting on the seventh, of the serpent, of the tree of life
and the tree of the knowledge of good and evil. Here we are given
an idyllic picture of a thornless, brambleless garden where there
is an always temperate climate, and work is pleasurable, and man
has dominion over the animals (that is the significance of the
man's naming them). Then there is the awareness of man and
woman being naked after having transgressed God's command,
and the fear of God and the flight from him. All these are
elements in an ancient story — and was there ever a story more
magnificently told than that in Genesis 3:1–13?

The elements in Genesis are, for the most part, taken over
from the myths of surrounding peoples, particularly, as we would
expect, from the Babylonians. But always these elements are
compounded in the story to present something quite special,
something to which the pagans had no access: God's revelation.

We have spoken of the accounts in Genesis as a story. Is this
to say that there is no *truth* in Genesis? Of course not. As we
have just seen, here is the deepest truth of all, God's own truth,
which comes to us in the form of ancient imagery.

Genesis is teaching us that God, the Unmade, is the sovereign
and undisputed Lord of all creation. He is not one deity among

many, not even the greatest of them. He is not a tribal god who runs the risk of being defeated when "his" tribe suffers military defeat. He is not a nature god like the Canaanite Baals whose control was limited to making the harvest grow or to bringing the rain. Everything which exists, material things included, depends absolutely on the one God. He creates and disposes as he wills, effortlessly.

Everything that comes from God is good, especially man. He is the summit of creation, breathed into, and living by the breath of God in whose very image he is made. His privilege is to commune with God, to worship him, and, as a sign of gratitude to him and dependence upon him, to rest on the sabbath.

Genesis clearly intends to convey that mankind's destiny must be seen as a whole. Mankind is one, a unity, despite its apparent disunity. This is a remarkable insight of the biblical author who, despite his limited geographical experience and historical memory, is able to teach us that mankind is a community in good and in evil. Each human being is responsible for all. It would appear that this profound theological idea has still to be assimilated by the race.

Sin is the violation of the order that God has established. First, it divides a man inside himself, and from this division no one is exempt. In every man's heart Paul's words find an echo: "For I do not do the good I want, but the evil I do not want is what I do" (Rom 7:19). Sin is not only in my situation, it is within me. Second, sin divides men from each other. The man blames the woman for his own guilt: he is quite prepared even to put the responsibility for his iniquity on his beloved wife. And the ultimate in sin's power to separate is murder.

Sin, then, is rebellion, disharmony, unfaithfulness. Sin is disobedience, a refusal to do God's will. This is why it entails being cut off from him who breathed life into us. By trying to establish his own criterion of good and evil in order to find enlightenment that way man is, in effect, trying to wrest God's sovereignty from him, to take from him his very divinity. (Hence the appropriateness of the incarnation when God's Son emptied himself. He who "was in the form of God, did not count equaltiy with God a thing to be grasped" [Phil 2:6]).

Sin brings shame and remorse. It means that man is a wanderer, in exile, on the earth. Its consequence is that man, the sinner, feels compelled to flee away from the one who made him and loves him because God is all-holy and he is not.

Genesis is also teaching that only God can redeem man from the mess he is in. Man may run away but God will pursue him, for he has a purpose for man and he will, as the Lord of history, bring that purpose to fulfilment. Genesis makes God's promise clear: he will be man's savior.

But who is the "man" of whom we have so far spoken? Whatever the influence upon mankind of some distant ancestor — and this question will be discussed later — the man in the story cannot only be someone who lived and died countless thousands of years ago. The man, Adam, is as well a mirror to the reader. Adam is myself for I am disobedient, hateful, unloving, rebellious. Adam is here and now; he is me and you and him and her. When King David was told by the prophet Nathan the story of a rich man who stole a poor man's solitary little ewe lamb to feed a traveler, he said: "As the Lord lives, the man who has done this deserves to die" (2 Sam 12:6). To David who had stolen Uriah's wife and saw to it that Uriah should be slain in battle, Nathan said: "You are the man." Genesis speaks to its every reader in like manner: "You are Adam, the man of dust." This is not to say, as we shall see below, that the Genesis story is simply a parable. But, then, neither was Nathan's story "simply a parable."

Enough has been said already to show the truth-value of Genesis. Genesis is a story and this is why it is inexhaustible in a way that a series of abstract statements is not. We can never scrap the book of Genesis on the plea that it contains outdated pictorial elements for these elements are the vehicle of God's revelation and we have no other. God's truth is contained there and this truth is inexhaustible. Genesis is like a quarry: we can never be sure that we have taken out of it all the true metal. We can never lay down a series of theological assertions and claim: "That is all that Genesis has to tell us." We have to express in ways accommodated to our age what the story means, but to say that we have grasped exhaustively what it means would be impertinence on our part. Hence we cannot, as some would have us do, throw the book of Genesis on the rubbish dump of outdated mythologies. Its message is endless.

Distinguishing the content and the vehicle of the message

It is plain today, though it was not plain a hundred years ago and less, that Genesis does not contradict science because it makes no strictly scientific assertions. It is teaching religious truth and not scientific truth and so it cannot be scientifically false. Father Schoonenberg writes:

> God's revelation is God's word by which he offers us his salvation. It is not a word in which he gives us knowledge of things that are irrelevant to that salvific message. God explains to us what he is for us and what we are for him. In this consists the whole content of God's revelation. It is not his intention to tell us things that we are able to discover by our human powers or to supply knowledge we are unable to obtain by these means . . . it does not intend to give us information that does not belong to our personal relationship with God. God does indeed speak to us about our final destiny and our origin. His revelation is both eschatological [about the last things] and "protological" [about the first things]. But eschatology does not supply prognoses for the future and "protology" does not make up for the gaps in paleontology.[1]

However, theology, in the past, has carved out of Genesis a series of propositions about Adam and Eve and their primeval sin. These are said to be theological truths and not scientific truths so called. How much of what is contained in Genesis is relevant to God's salvific message in Schoonenberg's sense? Every-

---

[1] *God's World in the Making* (Pittsburgh: Duquesne University Press, 1965), pp. 74–75.

thing. Nonetheless, we must try as far as we can to separate out the content from the means of expressing that content, otherwise we will, in fact, be in danger of mistaking outdated science for divine revelation.

In bygone centuries, for instance, Christians claimed that God took six days to create the world. Only a few fundamentalists claim that today. Until 1950 when Pius XII wrote his encyclical *Humani Generis* the majority of theologians would not countenance man's bodily origin from pre-human forms. They affirmed Genesis to mean that Adam was created immediately and perfectly by God. To deny this was considered by most scholars to be heretical (Some of their confirmatory arguments can only seem to us to be amusing — for example, that it would have been unbecoming for Eve to have originated from Adam's human rib if Adam himself had evolved, as far as his body goes, from a pre-human form of life). Today it is thought most probable that man's body emerged from animal forms.

Again, it is now generally agreed that when God is pictured as fashioning Adam out of the slime of the earth and breathing into him the breath of life this is but a way of expressing God's creative action and man's relationship to God. Man, though he is frail and part of the earth's substance, and though he is destined to pass back into the dust, is the summit of God's creation, living by God's own breath.

Think now of Eve. She is pictured as being moulded out of Adam's rib while he is asleep. This is surely not to be taken literally. Woman is part of a man's dream, as it were. She is as close to her husband as his own rib is to his heart. This is probably near to what the author intends to convey: the closeness and conjunction of man and woman in marriage, together with the basic equality of the sexes. These are great and fundamental truths, the latter pariculary being unknown to the pagans who downgraded woman in their society. Between man and woman exists the strongest and most permanent bond that can exist between God's children. In the Genesis story man and woman are depicted as *being* what in marriage they *become* — one flesh.

In other words the purpose of marriage — unity and union — is prefigured in the story wherein Eve is depicted as being fashioned out of a part of Adam's body.

Even when discussion turns to Adam and Eve, then, we are forced today to distinguish the truth of Genesis from the vehicle of presentation. We are forced, that is, to "demythologize" the story. This word, by the way, means "to get at the truth" not "to get rid of the truth" of the story.

But how far can this demythologizing process go? Could it be that Adam and Eve were not real historical individuals at all? If they were not, what becomes of original sin? Modern approaches to these questions will be outlined later. First it is necessary to give the usual presentation of original sin. Because it is already well known we can analyze it quite briefly.

The classical presentation of original sin

Adam and Eve were the first two parents of the race. From this couple all existing human beings are descended. They were created by God in the condition of divine sonship which was something beyond their due as creatures. They were endowed with the *supernatural* gift of sanctifying grace.

In their state of innocence Adam had other blessings from God called the *preternatural* gifts. They were immune, in the first place, from concupiscence which is that tendency to evil within us which is sparked off prior to our conscious deliberations and which reason must restrain. Adam and Eve's immunity from this weakness of ours is called the gift of integrity. In the Genesis story, the sign of this is the simple innocence they felt in their nakedness which contrasts strikingly with their shame after sin. When they sinned they experienced for the first time the rebellion of the lower powers of sense and imagination against the mind.

Adam and Eve, it is said, were also preternaturally free from the need to die. Death was the punishment for disobedience. The second chapter of Genesis is quoted as sufficient proof of this, and Paul corroborates it: "For if many (meaning "all") died through one man's trespass" (Rom 5:15) . . . The parallelism in St. Paul is: death through Adam and life through Christ.

According to classical theology, the first couple's possession of the gifts listed above is defined Catholic doctrine. The Council of Trent drew the threads of previous Councils together: it is the clearest, most synthetic presentation of the faith, and quite final.

Theologians went on to draw certain conclusions from Trent's teaching. Adam, it was inferred, was gifted with a singularly powerful intelligence free from the impediments of passion and sloth. The first couple were also credited with infused knowledge: they had from the beginning everything they needed to know to govern their lives well and to fit them for their responsibility as custodians of the graces of posterity. If they were unable to die, it was argued, surely they must have been free from all pain as well. (I can remember being told at school that Adam was not free from pain, for pain was of utility to the organism in warning it of impending harm. Adam was, however, free from "unpleasant pain!" This refinement of what was already a refinement has not yet ceased to amuse me.)

So the simple idyllic story of Genesis has been transposed into this more abstract and Western formulation. The creation is subject to man. In man, the lower faculties are subject to the higher, and the higher subject to God. The grace of God was dominant in Adam. It sanctified, ordered and harmonized everything within him. It percolated through the whole of his life, making him integrated as an individual and establishing him in peace with the rest of the animate and inanimate world.

Then came original sin, the fall. This was not simply the first sin of the first man but mankind's sin. Adam was something more than the first man, he was the head of all mankind. By sinning, our first parents lost the grace, the original justice in which they stood before God, both for themselves and for us.

Adam was guilty and so was punished. This sin of his was handed on to his descendants by generation. Not merely the punishment of sin or its consequences but the guilt of sin is ours. We are born in sin.

Of course, original sin in us must be sharply distinguished from any personal sins we may commit. The sin and guilt of original sin are not the same as the sin and guilt of actual sins. We are not in any way *responsible* for original sin; we do not do penance or make satisfaction for it; we are not strictly speaking "enemies" of God by reason of it. Many theologians were prepared to admit that if the mint of theological terms had been in their charge they would never have coined the term "guilty" for a child born in original sin: this is a very Pickwickian sense of guilty, indeed.

All the same, sin is essentially "godlessness." While to be born deprived is not to be born depraved it is to be born without grace nonetheless and so godless. In a word, every child who comes into this world is born in original sin, deprived of the supernatural life and deprived of the right to heaven. That the gifts of integrity and immortality were lost with grace was thought to need no elaboration.

Baptism is the sacrament of rebirth. We are born again when original sin which we inherited is washed away together with all the personal sins we may have committed. Henceforth, we are joined to Christ, the new Adam. Separated out from the man of dust (Adam), we live in and from the man of heaven (Christ).

Confronted with the question, "Is not the handing on of original sin unjust?" theologians made different replies. Sometimes it was said that this was no injustice because Adam's sin meant that we were only deprived of what, as creatures, we had no strict right to, in any case. The gifts we lost were not natural — if they were, they would have been due to us — but *super*-natural and *preter*-natural. This first reply was considered in every way unsatisfactory. Granted divine sonship is a free gift of God, it was to make us sons that God created us. Without such a gift wc cannot, in thc prcscnt ordcr, bccomc what God wants us to be: the purposes God inscribed in us cannot be realized. Without grace we cannot please God our Father nor live with him as his child everlastingly. Hence the charge of injustice is not yet sufficiently refuted.

A more impressive way to counter the charge of injustice, it was thought, is to appeal to Christ. Because of Christ grace is now available in greater abundance than before Adam sinned. This is what is meant when the Roman liturgy of the Easter vigil speaks of Adam's sin as "a happy fault which merited to have so great a redeemer." That liturgical text is a succint commentary on Paul's words: "If, because of one man's trespass, death reigned through that one man, much more will those who receive the abundance of grace and the free gift of righteousness reign in life through the one man Jesus Christ" (Rom 5:17). Unfortunately Paul did not tackle the problem of how *infants* were to receive this abundance of grace. It is a problem that is still, sometimes heatedly, discussed.

Difficulties arising from the classical presentation of original sin

We have now uncovered the bare bones of man's creation, elevation, and fall as they appear in classical theology. The difficulties connected with this classical structure have always been considerable. To some they appear today to have grown to unreasonable proportions. The views of these recent thinkers will be set out in later sections. Here we want to sketch some of the problems which were debated even before the more recent speculations on original sin.

Theologians were agreed on what the Council of Trent had laid down. Adam and Eve were the first parents of the whole race; they were created in grace with the gifts of integrity and immortality; everything was lost because of their sin; original sin was handed on by generation and not by imitation of Adam's sin; original sin is a real condition of godlessness needing remission by baptism or the desire for it. The special knowledge accredited to Adam, his freedom from (unpleasant) pain was not so widely held. In many circles it was considered speculation of a fairyland type. What follows is a brief selection from the many difficulties connected with doctrines generally considered to be defined.

What was the gift of immortality? Was it that humans were to live on endlessly? If so, how? Were they to live a kind of Peter Pan existence never growing old? Or was God's plan that people should grow old and get taken to heaven without that which we experience as the pangs of death? (Rahner suggests something like this and we shall quote what he has to say below.) Theologians were some while ago beginning to reject an ageless, Adonis-like Adam as a rather macabre idea hatched out of some mediaeval brain. However, two recent books show that the idea is far from dead. In *Christ Teaches Us Today* we read:

> God gave Adam the gift of freedom from death. And since Adam was free from death, he was also free from the causes of death: disease, accident and old age.
>
> Because Adam would never grow old, he would never suffer the weakening effects of old age. He would simply grow stronger and handsomer. A special providence of God protected him against anything that would harm him. Adam need never worry about germs or poisons. Accidents could not touch him.[2]

The author of *Jesus Christ, Lord of History* holds the same views and adds these remarks which are, one would have thought, singularly calculated to make Adam and Eve *personae non gratae* with the adolescents for whom he is writing:

> Without the labor of study Adam and Eve enjoyed the rewards of brilliant minds. They could understand the wonders of nature with a clarity that we never approach in our study of astronomy, physics, biology, and subjects like those; nor could they forget all that they knew as we so often do in our school work.[3]

[2] By M. J. Link, S.J. (Chicago: Loyola, 1964), p. 60.
[3] By V. M. Novak, S.J. (New York: Holt, 1964), p. 30.

It is hardly likely that the most gullible school child would be able to accept that Adam himself would have survived a head-on crash on the Jersey turnpike or that Eve knew her physics better than Einstein.

Further problems. In what sense can death be called "unnatural" in the present dispensation? Are not dissolution and death part and parcel of the world as we know it, the natural outcome of the friction of material things? If integrity and immortality were the consequence of grace why were they not restored with the superabundant grace of Christ? How otherwise could the restoration be said to be an improvement upon the original condition of man?

Why should sin be handed on? Why should all mankind be affected by the sin of one man? Or was it by the sin of Adam and Eve together? Ecclesiasticus 25:23 attributes sin to the woman as does Paul in 1 Tim 2:14: "Adam was not deceived, but the woman was and became a transgressor." (As Karl Barth remarked, the woman was the first to discuss theology.) In his letter to the Romans Paul speaks only of Adam as the transgressor and this has been the more common approach of theologians, though one wonders how much they were swayed in their opinion by an outdated biology which looked upon the male seed as the active cause of generation.

How exactly was Adam the "first man"? As the Queen is the first lady of the land by right of honor? Or was it because he was physically the first man? If this were so then a biological contingency was the determining factor in the flow of grace. And what would have happened had Adam and Eve not sinned but one of their children had? Would half the population have been born with grace and half without? Or was Adam the first man because God made a pact with him? This surely would betray a rather arbitrary attitude on God's part. It was thought hardly likely by those who held that Adam's mind had not the infused knowledge necessary to see all the consequences of his fault.

How was sin transmitted? If the soul is not handed on from parent to child but created immediately by God is not he responsible for creating something sinful?

What about babies dying before the age of reason, or, in the present dispensation, before they can be baptized? A child who dies in original sin, that is deprived of God's grace, cannot go to heaven. According to Augustine these children go to Limbo, the antechamber to hell, to receive the mildest punishment (*mitissima poena*). Other theologians in the early Middle Ages maintained that these babes were punished with hell's darkness, not with its fire and its worm. Others spoke only of the absence of the sight of God which strangely brings them no sadness. By the high Middle Ages the children are said to possess a perfect natural happiness. As Schoonenberg remarks: "The 'vestibule of hell' begins to look like a vestibule of heaven." Today's theologians, on the whole, tend to profess ignorance of what natural beatitude could possibly be like since we were not created for any such thing.

This, at least, is clear. A great change has taken place in the theology of Limbo since Augustine said the mildest punishment was meted out there. And Augustine has had considerable influence on the West's teaching on original sin. Another element in his writings has been quietly dropped: the tendency to identify original sin with concupiscence. This would make all sexual gratification even in marriage to some extent disordered. Officially this view is disapproved of by the Church, though, as we know, it still lingers in the Manichaean corners of men's minds.

New difficulties over original sin

Theologians have been perfectly aware of the problems mentioned above, and have done their best to grapple with them. In recent years new problems have arisen which are not simply additions to the old. They are of quite a different sort. I must apologize in advance for having to bracket together the theologians who have brought these problems to light, for in some respects they differ from each other both in their approach and in the strength of their assertions.

There are two main sources of recent difficulties over original sin, a more critical analysis of the Bible and a new world-picture given us by science. This world-picture is markedly different from anything that has gone before. Some theologians are claiming that a great number of theological statements in the past sprang not from revealed doctrine but from a now outdated world-picture buttressed by an antiquated biblical exegesis. In this section let us first give a broad presentation of their viewpoint before going into details and supporting arguments.

The idea of two primitive ancestors at the beginning of the human race, they say, is most unlikely.

The paradisial state of such a pair as shown in Genesis is really a projection, not a piece of history. The author is not affirming that such a blissful state existed in the past but that there will be a state like this in the future. "Perfection, fulfilment," writes Tresmontant, "are not behind us in a mythical Golden Age, in the past . . . ; they are before us, in the future, when the work of God, in which we are invited to co-operate, will be complete."[4] Schoonenberg says in an aside: "The 'paradise' of Genesis 2 is rather what awaits us than what we have lost."[5] Hulsbosch writes: "We must not evaluate this act of creation (by God) with reference to the beginning but with reference to the end."[6] Again, the same author: "The biblical account of the fall is a prophetic announcement about man and as such preserves for all time its value as revelation concerning the condition of man under God. But we cannot assign to the happenings in paradise any historical worth in the ordinary sense of the

---

[4] This and subsequent quotations are taken from an English translation by Mary Greenway of Claude Tresmontant's *La Doctrine Morale des Prophètes*, which in the event was not published. This is why no references can be given to quotations made. Thanks are due to Burns & Oates for permission to quote from this translation.

[5] *Concilium*, January, 1966, p. 33.

[6] A. Hulsbosch, *God's Creation* (New York: Sheed and Ward, 1965), p. 30.

words. No historical facts are related there, and we are not speaking about concrete persons."[7] Dubarle wholeheartedly agrees with this last sentence: "If history is understood as a detailed knowledge of certain facts in the past, based on testimony faithfully handed on by memory or by writing, then the historical character of the fall or of the whole of the early history can scarcely be maintained."[8]

It is important to keep in mind what these authors mean by "history" when they refuse to apply such a term to Genesis. They mean history in the modern sense. They would agree, I am sure, that in a broader sense Genesis is historical. Genesis is giving an account of the emergence of the present situation out of the past sins of the race. Its literary form is, therefore, less like a retailing of history as we understand it today than a judgment on history in the manner of the prophets and of Christ himself.

These authors are committed to showing or trying to show that their views are in accord with Catholic doctrine on original sin. How do their opinions square with scripture, tradition, the doctrines of the Councils (especially the Council of Trent) and the directives of recent popes, especially Pius XII's encyclical *Humani Generis?* I shall try to present the case for this group of recent theologians as fairly as I can, though the limits of this study demand a certain degree of selectivity.

An attempt at an intermediate view

Before examining in detail the sources of the new approach it is well to map out the general terrain a little better than has been done so far. These modern theologians — for so I shall call the above-mentioned group in this chapter for the sake of con-

---

[7] *Ibid.*, p. 51.

[8] J. Dubarle, *Biblical Doctrine of Original Sin* (New York: Desclée, 1965), p. 56.

venience — see themselves treading a path between two extremes.
For them the story of Adam and Eve is not merely a parable —
that would be a very superficial way of treating the Genesis
story — neither is it history in the modern sense. According to
Dubarle:

> There is room for an intermediate position, admitting the sche-
> matic and universal nature of the narrative but not missing the
> main point, a sin handed on by inheritance: what the text de-
> scribes is the effect of a countless multitude of individual sins. . . .
> Perhaps the theologians will agree to accept the idea offered them
> by biblical exegesis: the idea of a symbolic and schematic account
> intending to describe not a strictly individual event but a uni-
> versal condition passed on by inheritance.[9]

The reasons why Genesis cannot simply be considered a parable
are these. It is not enough to say that every person who comes
into the world finds himself in the same situation as Adam and
Eve in the story, faced with the same sort of trials and, in the
event, making the same sort of choices. We cannot look at Adam
and Eve and say: "I am in their kind of situation now." In a
way it would be true but it certainly wouldn't be enough to
explain the scriptures' and the Church's insistence on original sin
as mankind's sin. The parable interpretation gives the impression
that I myself, like Adam and Eve in the story, having come into
the world am required to tackle the promptings of evil on my
own and with a clean slate, so to speak. But this is precisely what
the doctrine of original sin is designed to avoid. We are not
isolated individuals, not Leibnizian monads, but men. We are
not cut off from mankind and the sinful history of mankind but
parcelled up with everybody else. The Bible, in considering men
as bodily beings, is teaching that all of them are linked together.
Together they constitute the chain of the generations. Men are
one by reason of a common origin, a common destiny and a
common iniquity.

Genesis is far more than a parable, it is in a certain sense
historical. The important lesson it propounds is that our sin
does not originate in us as individuals but in us as members of

---

[9] *Ibid.*, p. 226.

the race. Each of us is born into a sinful condition which deteriorates as time goes on. More than this, as we shall indicate below, the situation of sin affects us in our inmost being.

Besides the fact that we are born in sin, Genesis makes it plain that our own personal sin does not die with us. Each of us contributes to the sin condition of the race. For good or ill we affect those who come after us.

J. A. T. Robinson, the present Bishop of Woolwich, expressed well the time-conditioned — and, in that sense, the historical — character of sin in this lucid analysis of Genesis. This passage, though written in 1950, would, I feel, be acceptable to many of the modern Catholic theologians:

> Why then does the author place his characters in the first generation rather than in his own? Because he knows the dark mystery of that which he is trying to delineate. Sin is something that may not be understood in terms of one generation alone. Each person and every age knows that he or it is not wholly responsible. All men find themselves born into an historical order where sin is there before them, dragging them down. Go back into history as far as one may, one can find no generation and no civilization of which this is not true. There seems to be no time when sin was not there anticipating individual choice and decision. It is *not enough* to say that every man is his own Adam, because in this matter no-one starts from scratch. The Adam in us is bound up with the historical nexus into which each person is born; and so apparently has it always been. Consequently, in order to account for the condition of *present* humanity the author of Genesis makes his story tell of the first man and the first woman. It is essential that *in the myth* Adam and Eve shall be historical characters (and not, for instance, legendary heroes or demi-gods who have no place in the historical entail), and of historical characters the first. But it is a total misconception to imagine that the truth of the myth is in any way bound up with their being *actual* figures of history, or that it matters a scrap that as anthropology the whole thing is fantastic.[10]

There is here a stern repudiation of the shallow type of demythologizing of Genesis that sometimes went on in the past. Genesis is not a "myth" in the sense of teaching timeless truths in the manner of, say, a Buddhist parable. Its intent and its sig-

---

[10] *In The End, God* (London, 1950), p. 65.

nificance is historical — and this is why Adam and Eve are depicted not as an Olympian god and goddess but as a man and a woman embroiled in human affairs, indeed, as the initiators of human misery. However, Robinson no more wants to consider Adam and Eve as real individuals at the grass roots of history than as figures in a parable. Many Catholic theologians are in accord with him and science seems, they say, to confirm their view. Scientific findings make it impossible to accept the classical teaching on Adam and Eve. All are agreed that evolutionary processes have been going on for hundreds of thousands of years. Can the modern mind accept that these processes issued in a perfect man and a perfect woman who even from a bodily point of view must have been colossally different from everything before them; that from this couple the whole human race was meant to inherit special qualities of body and soul; that when Adam and Eve transgressed God's law their descendants, instead of continuing in the line which they had explosively initiated, went back to the normal dour evolutionary process as if Adam and Eve had never existed? Is it not easier to admit that they never did exist? The only alternative is to amuse every natural scientist worth his salt by claiming that Adam and Eve constituted a lightning interlude of complete perfection in the process of evolution which, when they sinned, went back to its long, slow, arduous uphill movement *toward* perfection.

The modern theologians themselves have found it impossible to swallow this. In setting forth their intermediate view they claim that it is to misinterpret Genesis and to contradict science to speak of Adam and Eve as real individuals. Their role in the story is a representative one. They are there to show the unity of the human race, the community in sin, the historical (or accumulating and so time-affected) condition of sin, and that each individual is born into this sin-laden condition. Original sin is what results in us by reason of our birth into this condition of sin which precedes our own personal and conscious choices and which inescapably affects us. From this, only God can deliver us.

This is the briefest and broadest account of the recent recast-

ing of original sin. There has been, until the time of writing, a
discernible growth in courage among the theologians responsible
for this more delicate venture. On the one hand, they are acutely
conscious that the faith must be understood against the back-
ground of the modern world-picture; that theology dies if it is
not so understood; that scripture must not be used any more to
"prove" pre-determined points of theology the concepts of which
depended more than was realized on an outdated scientific picture.
On the other hand, they want above all to be loyal sons of the
Church. This entails the refusal to jump on to the bandwagon
of new ideas just because they happen to be pleasant or attrac-
tive at the time. They know that whatever they put forward
must be reconcilable with scripture and tradition, and submitted,
in the long run, to the living teaching authority of the Church.
They take it for granted that we progress in our faith and that
dogma truly develops when new thinking is indissolubly linked
with the old. If they are, in other words, to interpret aright the
mythological elements in Genesis they know they must do so
with prudence, with infinite respect for the findings and expressions of scripture and the councils.

Let us now fill in the details of the landscape we have mapped
out by examining the two sources of the modern view, recent
exegesis and a changed scientific world-picture.

FIRST SOURCE OF THE MODERN VIEW
ON ORIGINAL SIN: EXEGESIS

The exegesis of Genesis

Since everything else in Genesis 1–3 has been demythologized
it seems strange that the same treatment has not been meted out
to Adam and Eve. Why should they stand out alone as historical
figures endowed with the extraordinary gifts accredited to them

by classical theology? Nobody holds nowadays as literal truth the six days of creation, the tree of knowledge of good and evil, the serpent, the fruit that got eaten, the description or location of the garden. These are mostly elements from pagan myths adopted by the author to give a new interpretation of human existence, an interpretation of the things which Israel had always puzzled over — pain, sin, death, the division of peoples. Were history in the exact modern sense being recorded there, it is unlikely that Genesis would have dressed it up in the "disguises" of pagans round about.

Even those theologians who hold the classical view that Adam and Eve are real individuals are bound to demythologize certain elements referring to them. Adam was not literally taken from the slime of the earth; Eve was not literally fashioned out of Adam's rib. Why not go to the end of the road and admit that Genesis is not history but a challenge in interpretation thrown to the pagans, the delineation of a new faith in God based on Israel's experience of God's intervention in their own history? Does not Genesis' novelty consist in its remarkable understanding of the sovereignty of God who has shown himself to be so good and faithful to his promises that the sin-situation can only be the product of man's refusal to live as God willed him to live?

Is not belief in the historical individual reality of Adam and Eve the last outpost of fundamentalism in their regard? Look what contradictions arise in an enlightened Catholic author, Bruce Vawter, when the wires of good exegesis and classical theology get crossed:

> Whether the author of Genesis believed that the human race began with only one man and one woman we do not know. He probably did. However, it cannot be shown that this forms part of the teaching of Genesis. The first account of creation, in fact, speaks of the origin of "mankind . . . Let them have dominion . . . male and female he created them . . ." While the second account describes one man and one woman, it does not insist on their individuality as creatures. . . . What is taught of the man and woman in this story as pertains to their human nature and qualities applies to all men and women, not to two only.

But Genesis most certainly teaches that one man and one woman were raised by God to a state above their nature, and that it is from this one man and one woman that the present human race is descended. That is the obvious sense of the following few chapters. Pius XII was only being faithful to the scripture when he decreed in *Humani Generis* that "the faithful . . ."[11] (here follows a quote from this encyclical which we will analyze below).

The author's discomfort is evident. Genesis, in his estimation, does not show that the human race began with one man and woman and yet it "most certainly teaches" that one man and one woman were graced by God and that from them the present race is descended. The two paragraphs quoted above might easily have been written by two persons, and the disharmony remains despite the qualifying phrase, "That is the obvious sense of the following few chapters." It is hardly likely, on the grounds of exegesis, that chapter four should see the beginning of a literary genre so very different from that of the chapters preceding it. It is certainly not "obvious" from Genesis that the human race descended from one man and one woman, as we shall proceed to show.

Take the semantic problem, that is, the problem of the meaning of words. The word in question is the Hebrew word "Adam." When it is not preceded by the article, it is transliterated in the Douai version so as to give the impression that it is a proper name. But the word "Adam" on the lips of a Jew meant any number of things. We cannot assume that when he used it he meant primarily an individual, "the first man," as we do. On the contrary, among the Jews the collective meaning predominated over the individual meaning. "Adam" stood mostly not for an individual, "the first man," but for "men" or "mankind" or, as we might say, "everyman." For example in the Book of Job we find: "Man that is born of woman is of few days, and full of trouble" (14:1). The word translated as "man" is "Adam." "Adam" comes from "Adamah" which is "earth" or "soil." Adam,

---

[11] Bruce Vawter, C.M., *A Path Through Genesis* (New York: Sheed and Ward, 1957), p. 62.

then, is man, the earthly, the man of the ground, the man of dust — and this is what all men are. (Likewise the word "Eve" is not a proper name: it means "life.")

As Father Vawter has indicated, this accounts for the otherwise extraordinary verse, Gen 1:26, where there is a change from the singular to the plural: "Let us make man (singular) in our image, after our likeness; and let *them* have dominion over the fish of the sea."

The word "Adam" might seem to represent "the first man" in Genesis 4 and 5 (as in Tob 8:6) where the author speaks of Adam begetting children by Eve and sets out the genealogies. But in what sense would the main run of scholars consent to see even here a reference to an *individual?* Is Adam an individual or is he not rather "a corporate personality," that is, a whole group of people designated by what appears to be a proper name? Even later on in Genesis where the author is dealing with events of history rather than of pre-history it is difficult to say whether he is talking of an individual or a tribe. To take a single instance: did Joseph, an individual, go down into Egypt and make good there or was it a whole group? In this case, is Joseph an individual or a corporate personality? The majority of scholars would no doubt choose the latter.

When we examine the genealogies of Genesis we find them very artificial constructions, indeed, and a part of a recognized literary form of the time. These genealogies were meant to show the solidarity of a race or a people in the gods' favor or disfavor and to bridge the gaps in history about which the author was perhaps totally ignorant. Likewise with Genesis. The names in Genesis 5 are names made up after the pattern of the Babylonian genealogies. In fact, the names which appear in pagan and Jewish genealogies are sometimes the same!

A further argument against the historical reality of an individual Adam and Eve is this: how would the author have known what occurred at the origins of the race countless centuries before his time? This information was not handed on either by written or oral tradition. Both hypotheses are absurd. Apart from the vast, intervening tracts of time, Abraham was the first of God's people among whom sacred traditions arose. His own ancestors had served "other gods" (Jos 24:2). In any case, the way Genesis depicts creation as static and not evolving proves its author knew nothing about man's origin or the world's.

It is always possible, naturally, to claim that the author was given a special revelation from God. A revelation of this sort, however, would be quite unique in the whole history of inspiration. Rather than adopt such an extreme hypothesis, it is asked, why not study an alternative which is so simple and so satisfying? Surely the author of Genesis is depicting, in a way which made sense to him and his contemporaries with their vivid sense of the solidarity of men, why mankind was so beset with troubles, why everyone was suffering from a sin-laden situation so evident and so terrible. He was not pontificating on how this situation had been brought about historically. However much he himself may have thought there was an original pair this was not, and could not, be a constituent part of his religious message.

This alternative to the classical position acquires force when we look at Genesis as a whole. At the time of the Flood, the animals went into the ark two by two in order to renew themselves two by two. This was the author's way of expressing the unity of each biological species. The suggestion is that Genesis 2–3 expressed in the selfsame way a truth which had deep theological implications, the unity of the human race. It is the theological truth of the unity of all mankind for God and before God and because of God's creative action which, according to modern theologians, is the important thing — not that the race is one by reason of its descent from two ancestors. This latter point is paleontology and not theology, and so is not strictly affirmed nor affirmable by the sacred author.

It has been further suggested that the Flood illumines the creation story in another way as well. The sin of Adam is depicted as having terrible consequences for his descendants. The purpose of the Flood was to wipe out iniquity over the whole earth. God, disgusted with the world's violence and corruption, says to Noah:

"I have determined to make an end of all *flesh*; for the earth is filled with violence through them; behold I will destroy them with the earth" (Gen 6:13). It was a clean sweep. "All flesh died that moved upon the earth . . . and every man" (7:21). "Only Noah was left, and those that were with him in the ark" (7:23). The destruction of the iniquity with which the earth was fouled since Adam being complete, only the clean, the just, were left. Mankind is reborn out of those few just men and women. This is a new Genesis (and, indeed, a foreshadowing of baptismal rebirth). There is, too, a new divine benediction which echoes the original blessing given to Adam and Eve in Genesis 1:28. Noah was told to leave the ark with his wife, his sons and their wives "that they may breed abundantly on the earth, and be fruitful and multiply and fill the earth" (9:1) and do no murder (9:6). The whole world had one language and few words (11:1), a sign of the unity of mankind.

Would it not seem that a Jew, reading Genesis as a single, straightforward story, would consider Adam responsible for the sin-situation only before Noah? Adam and Eve are made, in the story, to account for the original unity and the original disunity — but the disunity which now appears over the face of the earth dates back to the time of the Tower of Babel. For between Adam's sin and Babel, there had occurred the Flood which had wiped out all iniquity on the earth until then. (And, by the way, would Father Vawter say that "the obvious sense" of Genesis 6–10 is the literal and historical one?)

This, it has been concluded, may well explain why the traditions enshrined in the Adam and Eve stories had almost no impact on subsequent Jewish literature. In view of the predominant place Adam and Eve have held in Christian theology it is no less than startling to be told that in the whole of the Old Testament there are only a few scattered references to them. What a contrast this presents with the history of the patriarchs which is mentioned ceaselessly. Genesis 1–11 is, it has been said, a preface to history which really begins for Israel with the call of Abraham to be the father of God's people. It is pre-history in a poetic key. It is religiously of major importance in that it supplies an inspired biblical basis for our understanding of the whole historical process. It highlights key ideas such as the holiness of God, the unity of mankind, community in sin, hope in the outcome of history. But it is unlikely, on the grounds of an exegesis of Genesis alone, that we could hold with any assurance at all to "Adam" meaning the historically first man. Nor could we say that there is a hint anywhere in the Old Testament of an inherited sin as we Christians have been accustomed to think of it. The Jews certainly recognized — perhaps too realistically at times — the community of men in evil, what St. John referred to as "the sin of the world." (This notion of the sin of the world will be dealt with below.) They knew nothing of a sin handed on from parent to child.

The teaching of St. Paul

Paul never spoke of sin being handed on from parent to child by generation as Augustine did afterwards. But he is supposed to have elucidated and given a final, inspired interpretation of the Genesis story.

Paul is notoriously difficult to decipher and the letter to the Romans probably contains his most dialectical and, in places, his most obscure thought. I shall, therefore, be forced to deal more briefly than I would wish with the examination — never less than thorough — made by these modern theologians of his writings. Let us concentrate above all on Romans 5.

In this chapter, Paul contrasts Adam with Christ; the one is the origin of sin (not of all sin), the other is the origin of righteousness (all righteousness). This makes it clear that, continuing the thread of thought running through the whole of his letter, Paul is emphasizing God's love and the universal influence of Christ. Christ is uppermost in Paul's mind, not Adam.

Adam is, it seems, treated by the Apostle as a distinct individual. He speaks, for instance, of death reigning "from Adam
to Moses" (Rom 5:14). This was the interpretation current in
Paul's time, especially in aprocryphal writings (that is, writings
which were not part of the canonical or inspired scriptures).

Paul was a man of his time, just as Christ was when he spoke
of Jonah as being a sign to the men of Nineveh (Lk 11:30). Our
Lord referred to Jonah's stay in the whale's belly as foreshadowing his own resting in the dark tomb before resurrection (Mt
12:40). He made use of the Jonah story, he may even have assumed its literal truth, but he did not affirm it to be literally
true. In other words, that was not part of his teaching. Here the
question is: Did Paul simply think that Adam was a real, historical individual and make use of him as a parallel with Christ —
or did he affirm both that Adam was a real historical individual
and that his teaching on salvation depended on this fact? If the
latter is the case then all argument must cease, for whatever is
affirmed in this way in scripture, being God's own affirmation,
is "of faith." Has the Church, in whose province alone it is to
decide such matters, given a solemn and final answer to the question whether Paul is or is not making such an affirmation? Karl
Rahner who is a neutral witness in this debate claims in a most
carefully written chapter in his *Theological Investigations* that
the Church has not yet given a definite answer.[12]

In view of this, modern theologians have continued their examination of Paul with renewed vigor.

In Rom 5:12 Paul says: "Therefore as sin came into the world
through one man and death through sin, and so death spread
to all men because all men sinned. . . ." This death which is
said to have come into the world through sin is sometimes interpreted by modern theologians to be not biological death but
precisely the death brought about by sin. We will expound this
idea later on. Here we want to concentrate on this phrase: "Death
spread to all men *eph' hō* all men sinned." The two Greek words

---

[12] Chapter 8, "Theological Reflections on Monogenism," in *Theological
Investigations*, Vol. 1 (Baltimore: Helicon, 1961).

are translated as "because" in the Revised Standard Version. The Douai, keeping close to the Vulgate, has: "Death passed upon all men *in whom* all have sinned." The words *eph' hō* are translated as "in whom"; and this person "in whom" all men are said to have sinned was, according to Augustine, Adam. By understanding Paul to say "in whom (Adam) all sinned" Augustine influenced the whole of subsequent theology in Western Christendom. *There*, people have said, *is original sin*. Paul has expressed himself with unmistakable clarity: all men sin in Adam.

The only trouble with this from the exegetical point of view is that *eph' hō* does not mean "in whom"; and even if *eph'* meant "in" there still would be no reason for making *hō* refer to Adam ("the one man") whose name is mentioned two whole clauses before it in the sentence. Augustine was, in fact, the first person to translate the Greek as "in whom"; the Greek fathers never took it to be that. The most probable meaning of the relevant clause is as *The Revised Standard Version* has it: "Death spread to all men *because* all men sinned." The Jerusalem Bible translates: "Death has spread through the whole human race *because* everyone has sinned." Sin was in the world — it was "the sin of the world," the sin of mankind. This is what every individual now experiences prior to his own personal contribution to iniquity. But some exegetes think that Paul did not consider such sin except in respect of the personal sins committed by men. "Death spread . . . *because all men sinned*."

This seems a most reasonable suggestion. If one looks at the letter to the Romans as a whole one sees that Paul is dealing with the idolatries and iniquities of men, Jews and Gentiles alike. He was not concerned with what we would call original sin *in isolation*. He wanted to stress the breadth and abundance of all sin so as to bring out that grace has abounded even more. There is no evidence that Paul ever contemplated the situation of a baby born and dying in original sin. He was above all a preacher who theologized, not a theologian who preached. He was concerned with the sin which is in the world and in men, which has accumulated throughout the ages, and which men

by their own personal sinful choices connive at and collude with
— not with the state of babies who never came to hear him
preach. He even writes — and this passage could well be applied
to the case of infants: "Apart from the law [which brings the
knowledge of sin] sin lies dead. I was once alive [before the
knowledge of the law] apart from the law, but when the commandment came [which men are too weak to keep] sin revived
and I died" (Rom 7:8–9).

The realization that the New Testament (like the Old) speaks
of sin in reference to adults shows that a catechesis of sin should
begin with them and not with babies. Likewise with baptism.
Baptism is necessary for all after Christ's crucifixion; we are born
in mankind's sin; we all need to die with Christ and be reborn
with him; we all have to be snatched out of "the world" and
come to live in the community of grace, the Church. Nonetheless,
if we follow the New Testament we cannot but be aware that the
exemplar of baptism is not infant but adult baptism. This remains
true however early infant baptism made its appearance in the
Church — it was general even by the first half of the second century — and despite the fact that there are more babies baptized
today than adults.

Infant baptism is not thought out at all in the scripture because
sin in their regard is not contemplated either. Baptism in scripture has solely in view the man who has experienced the weakness
and the "twistedness" within himself, who has actually sinned
despite not wanting to, who sees his life petering out in emptiness, meaninglessness, futility, who wants to receive the power
to live and to love from on high, who is prepared for a total
change of heart. Baptism is, therefore, dealt with in the New
Testament as a matter of conversion, repentance. To be baptized
one has to turn one's back on iniquity and come to Jesus the
Lord and the Savior in the community of salvation which he
established.

A baby cannot be "dead" in the same sense as a sinful adult
is "dead" in his actual sins. This is perhaps the force of Paul's
words: "Death spread to all men because all men sinned." This

is certainly the reason why the Church teaches that no infant can taste "the second death," that is, no infant can suffer the pangs of hell which follow upon the final impenitence of one who has refused to love God more than himself.

The catechesis on both sin and baptism should begin with Acts 2, where Peter, on the day of Pentecost, is reported to have called on his fellow Jews to repent of their personal iniquity and come to Jesus in whom alone we find salvation and fulfilment.

The scriptures on sin and death

Classical theology maintained that Adam and Eve, had they not sinned, would not have died. Modern theologians, while acknowledging the close connection between sin and death, are inclined to interpret the biblical doctrine of death and freedom from death as set out in Genesis rather differently.

Karl Rahner, while disagreeing with the modern theologians, was himself busy modifying to some extent the classical position in an attempt to make it more acceptable to our contemporaries. Before sin, Adam was not subject to death. He continues:

> It is not legitimate, however, to infer from this proposition of faith that the first man in Paradise, had he not sinned, would have lived on endlessly in this life. Rather can it be said with certainty that he would surely have experienced an end to his life, but in another manner; maintaining the integrity of his bodily constitution, he would have conducted this life imma- nently to its perfect and full maturity.[13]

Rahner speaks of an end to man's life on earth, an active consummation of the whole man, "a death without dying," as he puts it. What interests us here is his conviction that Adam's immortality did not entail that he would have grown handsomer each day or passed an endless, unchanging sort of existence. His life would have terminated even in Paradise.

---

[13] *The Theology of Death* (New York: Herder & Herder, 1961), p. 42.

The modern theologians, while accepting "the proposition of faith" that before sin mankind is not subject to death, nonetheless affirm that man of his nature is destined to die. They claim that what Genesis meant by death is the death of sin, not biological death. What results from sin is not death as a natural process of dissolution but death as a state of rebellion and alienation from God, that is death not as biological but as theological. Between sin and physiological death, the Bible, it is affirmed, does not put a bond of cause and effect: the death of the body is a natural necessity, not a punishment. What is new after sin is the changed relationship in which man stands to God.

If Genesis is read with fresh eyes and without the presuppositions of classical theology we see that it is Adam's (that is, man's) nature to be dust. We read, too, how God said to the man: "Of the tree of the knowledge of good and evil you shall not eat, for in the day that you eat of it you shall die" (Gen 2:17). It is on the very day of his disobedience that Adam dies. What does that death consist in? The serpent tempted the woman with: "You will not die . . . you will be like God, knowing good and evil" (3:4, 5). Deathlessness is being like God, having God's prerogatives. Death, therefore, consists in being unlike God, and, in effect antagonistic toward him. Contrary to the serpent's insinuations, it is not possible to be like God by disobeying him: that way leads to death. To "die" is not to return to dust. That is man's nature to be dust — "you are dust" (3:19) — and it is his destiny to return to it (cf. Ecclus 17:1). "Real" death, biblical death, so to speak, is sin-laden death; it is returning to dust alienated from God through disobedience.

Is this so-called biblical death truly biblical? Let us look at a sample of texts:

> "See," said Moses to Israel, "I have set before you this day life and good, death and evil. If you obey the commandments of the Lord your God which I command you this day, by loving the Lord your God, by walking in his ways, and by keeping his commandments and his statutes and his ordinances, then you shall live and multiply. . . . But if your heart turns away, and you will not hear, but are drawn away to worship other gods

and serve them, I declare to you this day, that you shall perish. . . . I have set before you life and death, blessing and curse; therefore choose life, that you and your descendants may live, loving the Lord your God, obeying his voice, and cleaving to him; for that means life to you and length of days" (Dt 30:15–20).

The soul that sins shall die (Ezek 18:4).

Seek the Lord and live (Amos 5:6).

Before men are life and death. Whichever they choose is given them (Ecclus 15:16).

Biological death is not an option; it is the death of sin that men can choose. The New Testament has exactly the same outlook.

When the commandment [of the law] came sin revived and I died (Rom 7:9).

If you live according to the flesh you will die, but if by the Spirit you put to death the deeds of the body you will live (Rom 8:12).

You, he [God] made alive, when you were dead through trespasses and sins but God . . . even when we were dead through our trespasses, made us alive together with Christ (Eph 2:1, 4, 5).

In the days of his flesh, Jesus [prayed] to him who was able to save him from death, and he was *heard* for his godly fear (Heb 5:7).

If anyone keep my word he will never die (Jn 8:31).

In all these texts the death spoken of is the death of sin, as the life referred to is living to God in Christ. When Christ's prayer to be saved from death is said to have been "heard," it was heard insofar as God saved him not from death as such but a meaningless death by raising him on the third day. When John speaks of our passing by faith from death to life he means not from biological death to bodily life, but from the deepest death there is, which is godlessness, to a god-filled life.

Tresmontant concludes:

In the whole of biblical tradition, death is considered as a "natural" fact, and no biblical writer ever explains the death of the body as an effect of man's sin. . . . We are not forced to believe that, without sin, individual human beings would have been immortal.

He goes on to say that many people cannot see this and so "interpret these essentially theological texts on a plane which is alien to them: namely the empirical one of history and biology." Likewise Dubarle:

> To be faithful to the statements of Genesis and St. Paul we do not need to postulate a corporal existence immune from decease. The inspired authors saw a consequence of sin in these tragic experiences surrounding death (physical sufferings, family separation and a feeling of hopeless failure). They did not speculate explicitly on what a state of innocence would have been like or on the possible dissociation between physical decease and death as the sum of human ills.
>
> The magisterium of the Church has made no irrevocable pronouncement on this point.[14]

According to these authors, after sin man is not simply condemned to die, he has died. He still walks the earth but as a dead man. This is a paradox which is paralleled in the case of "life." When we are reborn, even though we must some day die, we are alive and beyond the touch of death. Death (biological death) will not have dominion over us because it is endowed with new significance by reason of our baptism. When we were baptized we died the only death that mattered, death with Christ to sin. For men who sin and for men who are justified death is a reality and sometimes immensely painful. But for each group it has a different significance.

Schoonenberg in *Man and Sin* writes:

> It is perhaps possible to modify the classic doctrine in such a way and to understand its statements in such a manner that biological death is modified anthropologically, that it acquires another meaning for man.[15]

The same author writes in an equally probing yet uncertain manner in *God's World in the Making*: "Is it possible to interpret the entry of death into the world not as implying a change in man's nature but in his personal attitude towards death?"[16] If so, then it becomes less important that we look upon the Adam

---

14 *Op. cit.*, p. 234.
15 Sheed and Ward, 1965, p. 183.
16 P. 103.

and Eve story as a precise incident at a precise moment of time.

The views outlined in this section have been current in non-Catholic circles for a considerable time. Gabriel Hebert in a recent work expresses how alien to most of our contemporaries is the classical teaching on Adam and Eve and original sin.

> It has often been assumed that "death" means the death of the body, and those who have taken the story of the Fall as "literally true" have believed that man before the Fall was immortal; this, however, is impossible for us to take seriously, since we know that Man has evolved from lower forms of life, and death is universal in the animal creation. . . . Actually in the story that which happens to Man is something much worse than bodily death. That which dies in him is his manhood. . . . "The mind of the flesh is death," for "the mind of the flesh is enmity with God" (Rom 8:6–7).[17]

> . . . the name "Adam," meaning "Man," and the name "Eve," meaning "Life," show that the Man and the Woman are not being thought of merely as individuals in history. Their sin is the sin of Man; and as the whole pattern of the story shows, that which is being described is the passing of Man from a right relation to God (dependence, thankfulness, obedience) to a wrong relation (independence, rebelliousness, alienation). Man chooses to live without God.[18]

SECOND SOURCE OF THE MODERN VIEW ON ORIGINAL SIN: A NEW SCIENTIFIC WORLD PICTURE

The world picture of yesterday and today

The modern theologians whose opinions I am outlining claim that the past presentation of original sin has been determined by the world picture of Genesis. This world picture has been blown

---

[17] *The Old Testament From Within* (London: Oxford University Press, 1962), pp. 21–22.
[18] *Ibid.*, p. 25.

sky high since the nineteenth century, especially since Darwin. Despite this evident fact, many elements of that picture remain in the presentation of original sin even today. These elements will have to be eliminated if Catholic doctrine is going to be satisfactorily presented to modern man. The author of Genesis would have made no impact on his readers if he had put forward his teaching according to an evolutionary world picture; we, in our turn, will leave our own contemporaries cold if we present Genesis' teaching according to a static world picture.

We have to be clear on this: the evolutionary image of the world is the only one that makes sense to our contemporaries. It is of no use for us to complain that they do not believe the message we bring them if we insist on couching it in terms and conceptual structures which appear to them decidedly primitive. They are, as a consequence, never confronted with Christian doctrine because they are put off in advance by concepts alien to all their thinking. We know that preaching (and evangelization) to be effective needs to have more than truth on its side. For this truth to break through the thick crust of skepticism surrounding modern man it must have a reasonableness about it.

There is a difference between Christian ministers and theologians adopting the latest "fad" which will pass in a month or a year — for instance, introducing the latest pop-tunes or dances into liturgical celebrations — and adopting the very thought forms and processes without which we would not be men of our times at all. History shows that Christians have too often been behind the times in accepting the inevitable. We have only to think of the Galileo incident or the once wholesale rejection of Freud or, the case in point, the repudiation of Darwin's findings. John L. McKenzie tells us:

> A few years ago a theologian made a survey of theological manuals written in 1880–1900. He found that of some twenty five manuals all but three or four censured the theory of evolution as heresy. Did these men serve the Church better than those who denied that the theory is heresy?[19]

[19] *Myths and Realities* (Milwaukee: The Bruce Publishing Company, Chapman, 1963), p. 6.

It might be argued that the Church is of necessity somewhat behind the times because she has to be absolutely convinced that a change of world-picture in presenting the faith does not lead to the loss of a single iota of revealed truth. There is something in this, and it may explain to a large extent why Thomas Aquinas was posthumously condemned for his introduction of Aristotelian philosophy into scholasticism. Our faith is historical, and it advances in strict continuity with the past, linked forever with its apostolic origins. The Church must, for truth's sake, walk warily when others plunge foolishly in. Whereas some, a select few, reach truth before her and show her the way, multitudes embrace the most dangerous falsehoods from which she keeps distantly aloof. Mothers, after all, are notoriously careful where the safety of their children is concerned. We must, on the other hand, be on our guard lest the carefulness of Mother Church be confused with the stubbornness, even bigotry, of unreflecting theologians. Certainly we must no more impose needlessly — if it be needlessly — an outdated world picture on prospective converts than Jewish circumcision and ritual.

What light, then, does modern science cast on the Church's teaching on original sin? Does science help us to make explicit what is revealed to us by God and to separate out this revelation from the pictorial clothing which covers it? (We have seen that this has happened already to a certain extent. Our predecessors, mistaking pictorial elements for articles of faith, felt quite convinced that God literally took slime of the earth and fashioned Adam out of it.) Does science suggest a new way of presenting the Church's teaching on original sin which is more accommodated to the modern mentality?

First, what has science to tell us about the origin of man? Does it hold the descent of man from one couple or many couples? — the technical terms for the two views are monogenism and polygenism respectively.

Science cannot say definitely that mankind arose from many couples. Monogenism cannot be absolutely ruled out. But the spontaneous assumption of scientists as scientists, in accord with the acknowledged norms of evolution, is that the human race evolved from numerous couples. This assumption is very widespread in the academic world. It carries much weight with one who may otherwise be sympathetic toward Catholicism. He is puzzled when he is presented with the story of Adam and Eve and their sin as a literal historical truth rather than as a piece of folklore with theological relevance. He might so much more easily accept the account as *theologically* significant.

The suggestion that the first members of the human race actually possessed the preternatural gifts of integrity and immortality appears to the scientist, as we would expect, to be a most amusing hypothesis. The first men, most of our contemporaries believe, were born not of humans at all but of animals. They consider that Michelangelo's representation of Adam's marvelously proportioned and beautiful body on the ceiling of the Sistine Chapel must be recognized for what it is: the product of a superb artistic imagination under the spell of a non-evolutionary science and theology. When they refer to the first men their imagination is peopled with Neanderthal and Pithecanthropus and such creatures. Hence Hulsbosch, vividly aware of the contrast between classical theology and modern science, writes:

> It is difficult to accept that the human race originated in a pair of human beings, which had been given the spiritual and bodily qualities which are traditionally attributed to Adam and Eve before the fall. One would rather expect, in this dim beginning, types which hardly emerged from the animal stage.[20]

Furthermore, a first man's bodily condition would have been related to his surroundings. A perfect bodily condition would have required paradisial surroundings and been in its turn the pre-requirement of a perfect spiritual condition. In other words, because of man's psycho-somatic nature the spiritual state would have depended upon the bodily state, and the bodily state upon paradisial surroundings. These last — the basis of the rest — have been demythologized so that the other elements of classical theology seem to have lost their support.

---

[20] *Op. cit.*, p. 27.

The most important objective, argue the modern theologians, is to bring into the presentation of theology the conceptual structures o four age. Genesis presents a static world picture. Its presupposition is that everything was created perfect, and that as things now are so were they in the beginning. This is its presupposition. It does not teach, for example, that man was created in a trice out of the slime of the earth. That is a scientific matter. The author may have supposed it to be the case but one could scarcely list it among his "teachings."

Today's presupposition — and it is confirmed by innumerable discoveries — is that man was not created directly out of the dust as depicted by Genesis but that he evolved out of the dust and through intermediate forms over hundreds of thousands of years.

Because of his world picture the author of Genesis, we repeat, makes everything quite perfect from the start, the first birds, each in their kind, the progenitors of today's birds, the first humans the progenitors of today's humans. Knowing nothing of evolution and overwhelmed by God's goodness and man's iniquity he portrays a perfect past of the human race, a paradisial condition from which man has fallen through his own fault.

Our world picture is dynamic and evolutionary; it is not genesis in the biblical fashion but cosmogenesis in the scientific fashion. Hence we cannot accept the perspectives of the Adam and Eve story as classically presented. God's world is *in the making*. That is its nature: to be a world in process of becoming. Our attention is automatically attracted not to what things once were long ago but to what they are to be, not to the beginning but to the end. Paradise, it is said, is not at the commencement of historical process but at its consummation. The paradise-state is not a description of a past situation but a hope of what is to come. Put in another way, the paradise-state depicts how we stand *essentially* before God though this essential condition has to be slowly, hence *historically* realized in us through God's saving action.

According to Tresmontant:

> The bible's view of history looks forward. In the bible, the only person who looks back is Lot's wife. The hopes, the wishes

and the efforts of the prophets of Israel are all directed towards the completion of God's work, which St. Paul terms the *pleroma* — fulness. The redemption is not simply atonement, it is also creation: God creates a new humanity, and man is asked to consent to this new birth which will make of him a new creature, a new man.

From this quotation, which is not untypical of the modern theologians, we see that the final demythologization of Genesis is looked upon as a quite necessary step if theology is to be recast according to the intellectual requirements of our age. It is to be recast by presenting redemption as basically creation as well as atonement. Christ did not come simply to repair sin but to bring the creation which began in imperfection to fulfilment.

A word of warning is in place here. Whilst these modern theologians speak a great deal about the Bible's orientation toward the future they, above all, hold that it is necessary to look back upon man's sin. They believe in "original sin," the sin of mankind. They want to set forth the whole wide sweep of the race's iniquity. This sinful state is prior to our own personal decision — it is "within us" in a manner to be explained below. From this state in which we are powerless to do good we need to be redeemed, and in fact are redeemed by Christ the sole Savior of mankind.

Before we examine the enthralling task that modern theologians claim to have initiated, namely, a considerable recasting of theology, we have to see how they encounter the charge made against them that their views cannot be reconciled with the official teaching of the Church.

The teaching of Pius XII in Humani Generis

Pius XII was the first pope to deal ex *professo* with original sin in the light of modern scientific research. He allowed the possibility of man's bodily origin from lower prehuman forms as a result of which manuals had to be altered. But what was his teaching on the descent of the human race from a single couple or a "people"?

Polygenism he termed "a conjectural opinion," that is, nothing more than a scientific hypothesis. As to its connection with theology he maintained that the faithful could not hold the theory that after Adam there existed on this earth true men who did not take their origin from him, the first parent of all, by natural generation. Nor could they hold that "Adam" stood for a people, a multitude. His reason was:

> Because it is in no way clear how this view can be reconciled with those things which the sources of revealed truth and the acts of the Church's magisterium propose about original sin, which is the result of a sin truly committed by an individual Adam and which being handed on to all by generation is within each person as his own (*Humani Generis*, sect. 37).

At first sight, this would seem to the untheological reader to be a categorical denial of polygenism, a reaffirmation and consolidation of the classical view of original sin. But apart from the fact that *Humani Generis* is a pastoral decree suited to its time things are not so simple as all that.

Karl Rahner has analyzed the key passages of Pius XII's encyclical in detail in his essay "Theological Reflexions on Monogenism."[21] The conclusion he comes to is that monogenism is "theologically certain," a strong qualification requiring that we give to monogenism an internal assent. (Since a statement which is "theologically certain" is not unrevisable nor even *irreversible*, the word "certain" is evidently used in a way quite contrary to its usages in ordinary discourse.)

Rahner's testimony is all the stronger in that he himself holds most firmly to the truth of monogenism for a number of reasons. He points out that Pius XII did not say that polygenism is heretical, as did most theologians prior to *Humani Generis*. Pius XII said *it is not clear* how polygenism can be reconciled with what the sources of revealed truth and the acts of the magisterium

---

[21] *Theological Investigations*, Vol. 1, Ch. 8.

have proclaimed. There, sin is spoken of as the sin of an individual, handed on by generation and within each person as a consequence.

It is certainly not clear and immediately obvious that any reconciliation is possible; and a Catholic is not free to peddle any opinion he wishes regardless of whether it can be harmonized with the traditional teaching of the Church.

Pius XII did not affirm nor did he deny that future reflection and research might bring polygenism into line with traditional teaching. In the years following *Humani Generis* some theologians, at first gingerly then with increasing assurance, were suggesting that historical research and theological reflection in the light of scientific presuppositions and discoveries made it possible to affirm that polygenism was not irreconcilable with Catholic doctrine. They were thankful that Pius XII did not censure polygenism as heresy. In fact, they pointed out that he had not quoted a single document (say, from Trent) nor a single verse from scripture (say, from Romans 5) as proof that the matter was already beyond dispute. In short, Pius XII didn't open the door to polygenism. If anything, he was himself personally in favor of closing the door to polygenism. Nevertheless, he certainly didn't lock the door.

Tackling the statements of classical theology

The stage seemed set, then, for a re-examination of the statements of classical theology on original sin. The first thing the modern theologians had to do was to lay down the general strategy to be followed. Briefly, it amounted to this: the decrees of councils must be looked at as are the books of the Bible themselves, *in their historical context*. Outside that context we are more than likely to misunderstand what the councils are teaching us.

Any Christian who takes everything he reads in the scriptures in literal fashion we call a fundamentalist. We must beware of a fundamentalist approach to the councils.

It is worth remembering that council statements are derivative. The scriptures are, in a more primary sense, the word of God and only they are inspired. The council statements are expositions of this word, clarifications and definitions. They are not the "last" word — the scripture is that already — but clearly enunciated, precise, limited (that is what "defined" means) statements based on scripture. Such definitions are irreversible (as all truth is) and yet accommodated to the particular age for which they are made. On the one hand, it follows that we cannot in subsequent ages ignore these definitions. They are an exact, true enunciation of what scripture means, so that when we read the scriptures today we cannot, for instance, forget the Church's solemn profession of faith in the divinity of Christ and the Spirit. On the other hand, there is another possible danger, that of thinking that what the Church has said in council or creed has not merely defined the word of God but exhausted its potential. It is remarkable how often in the past a definition of the Church has been equated with an exhaustive analysis of a particular aspect of Christian truth. Equally remarkable has been the reluctance to apply to conciliar documents principles generally accepted in regard to the scriptures. For instance, we have to examine the time-conditioned character of conciliar documents. We have to put them in their literary, theological and historical contexts. We have to acknowledge the possibility of scientific research casting fresh light upon them. New questions arise with new circumstances. It is foolish to think that past councils can provide us with answers to such questions when they were not, and could not possibly have come, under consideration at that time.

We must not confuse, either, the assumptions of the council fathers with their affirmations. In all men's minds there are assumptions below the explicit or implicit affirmations that they make. These affirmations will often stand when the assumptions have been exploded. This principle is as applicable to conciliar documents as it is to the scriptures. Let us not think that a position universally held in christendom is necessarily of faith. It may be simply one of these unquestioned, and, in previous ages unquestionable, assumptions. There was perhaps not the slightest reason for doubting it but this is no reason for claiming that it was the universal teaching of the Church.

An example of how the general principles just enunciated are applied in a particular instance may be of value.

The Council of Trent states:

> If anyone does not confess that the first man Adam, when he had transgressed the commandment of God in paradise, immediately lost his holiness and the justice in which he had been established . . . and that through that offense of prevarication the entire Adam was transformed in body and soul for the worse, let him be anathema.[22]

In this sample statement Trent seems to have in mind an individual ("the first man Adam") initially established in a paradisial state and whose sin affected him personally for the worse in body and soul. This sin affects us, too, for we, his descendants, inherited not merely the punishments of the body but sin (the death of the soul) as well. This sin of Adam is one in origin (*unum origine*). It is transmitted to all and is in each one as his own "by propagation and not by imitation."[23]

It might be asked: "Isn't the message clear enough? How could it be doubted that here the Church is solemnly proclaiming monogenism? Here we are surely being taught that there was one couple at the fount of the race, and their sin is handed on by bodily generation."

However, as was said above, if things were really so clear why did not Pius XII simply repeat Trent? Why did he not say that this question was finally settled in the sixteenth century and that to deny monogenism is heresy?

He did not do this for the simple reason that Trent had no intention of *affirming* monogenism to be Catholic truth. This

---

[22] Denzinger, 788.
[23] *Ibid.* 790.

was their assumption. It was not something that entered anybody's mind, Catholic or Protestant, at the time of Trent to
question or deny.

If it was an assumption the problem arises: is it a true assumption? Is it a necessarily true assumption if the doctrine of original
sin is still to be taught by the Church? In other words, although
not explicitly defined, was monogenism implicitly defined by
Trent? All we have to go on at the moment is that in 1950 Pius
XII, although pressed to do so, did not say that monogenism is
defined, only that it is not clear how polygenism can be reconciled with the Church's teaching on original sin.

Attempts to reconcile polygenism with original sin

Modern theologians have been claiming since 1950 that the
Church's teaching on original sin does not entail the belief that
there was a single couple at the origin of the race. This was not
implicitly defined by Trent but assumed; and the assumption is
not in harmony with today's scientific findings of which the
Council fathers naturally knew nothing. The truth about original
sin can and must be maintained even when the pre-scientific
assumption of a single couple (Adam and Eve) is repudiated.
"Belief" in Adam and Eve was once thought to be the necessary
safeguard of belief in original sin and the only way to account
for its transmission. Today, such a belief in Adam and Eve is
scientifically untenable and theologically superfluous.

Trent did not merely teach original sin. In teaching it, the
Council reproduced the picture of Genesis. The picture was not
strongly criticized until the nineteenth century and the advent of
evolutionary theory. The fact that the picture of a single couple
at the fount of the race was assumed for nineteen centuries does
not mean that the Church taught it. There were many other
elements in Genesis which were also assumed for the same length

of time, such as man being created from the earth's slime and Eve coming from Adam's rib.

How are we to deal with the Church's formula that sin is one in origin and is handed on by procreation and not by imitation? We must look beyond the form of words to the message conveyed by means of it. We must ask: What is the Church *teaching* us by that and similar phrases?

"One in origin," so the argument goes, is only a simple, abstract way of expressing what Genesis means when it tells, in story form, of Man and Woman at the roots of the human race. Trent is not teaching any more or any less than the author of Genesis. "One in origin" is a sixteenth-century Western way of expressing what a semite had expressed centuries earlier in an unforgettable story. There had been no change in scientific picture in the intervening years; no scientific data were available to the fathers of Trent to suggest that the Genesis picture was "dated."

The historical context of Trent warrants more interest than it usually receives. The fathers of the Council, with the author of Genesis, would never have dreamed of asking: "Is it possible to reconstruct the past?" Had the fathers of Trent been told that the long distant past could one day be reconstructed this would have seemed far more shattering to them than anything Galileo was to say about the solar system. We know what Pope Paul V's reaction was when in 1616 Cardinal Allesandro Orsini spoke to him circumspectly and prudently of Galileo's "Copernican Opinion": "The Pope tol dhim it would be well if he persuaded him (Galileo) to give up that opinion. . . . As soon as Orsini had left, his Holiness summoned Bellarmine, and, after brief discussion, they decided that the opinion was erroneous and heretical."[24] That the curtains of ancient time would, in centuries to come, be drawn aside to reveal its secrets would doubtless have appeared to the Qualifiers (theological experts) of the Holy Office quite as worthy of condemnation as Galileo's claim

[24] Words of the Tuscan Ambassador to Duke Cosmo II. Quoted in Arthur Koestler, *The Sleepwalkers* (Penguin, 1964), p. 461.

that the wholly immovable sun is the center of the world. The "paleontological opinion" would also have seemed:

> foolish and absurd, philosophically and formally heretical inasmuch as it expressly contradicts the doctrine of holy scripture in many passages, both in their literal meaning and according to the general interpretation of the fathers and doctors [of the Church].[25]

One could even have sympathized somewhat with them in their anathematizing. The past, after all, was past. Of the recent past, witnesses might remain to tell the tale. But of the very distant past no knowledge was possible. The past was not "that sort of thing."

The deeply ingrained conviction that the past was only a matter of conjecture obviously affected the way the ancients wrote up "the past." If it had been suggested to the author of Genesis that three thousand years after his death men would know more about what had happened thousands of years before his own time he would not have paid much heed. Nor would the fathers of Trent.

We are, in scientific matters, more enlightened. We even presume that in the future our knowledge of the distant past will improve. We cannot pretend that our presuppositions about the origin of the race are the same as those at the time of Trent or that we can accept the part of Man and Woman in the Genesis story at its face value. Adam and Eve are not strictly historical as we understand that term with our entirely different conception of history and our entirely different optimism about the possibilities of uncovering the past.

Trent and Genesis were not making historical statements beyond the possible scope of their contemporary knowledge. By their diverse formulations they were both teaching the unity of the human race. Today some theologians are asking: "Is it necessary, in order to keep the unity of the race, to maintain descent from a single couple? Is not the human race one because it is created by God, and created by him for Christ (Col 1:16)?

---

[25] *Ibid.*, p. 462.

Are we not one because God intends us all to be brothers of Christ (Gal 3:28)?"

What are we to make of the statement that all men inherit sin "by propagation and not by imitation"? Here the contrast is the important thing: by propagation and *not by imitation.* Trent is teaching, as was Genesis, that there is an inheritance of sin, that men do not become sinners simply by copying Adam. The Adam story, as was explained above, cannot be written off as a parable. Men are born into a state of guilt they inherit from their predecessors, a godless situation from which only God can deliver them. He does deliver them because of Christ who is all men's Savior.

This, it is claimed, is the positive intent of Trent's phrase, "by propagation not by imitation." Men, even apart from their personal sins, are born into a grace-less state, a state of sin. Genesis clearly taught that there was a connection in sin between the generations. What the author depicts as some undefined connection by generation (physiological origin) the modern theologians wish to widen so as to include the social and psychological influences as well as the biological. Sin, they consider, is less like a torch being handed on than like a snowball accumulating or like a chain-reaction spreading or like a complex network of interrelating threads. They would approve not so much of a sin by generation — with all its Manichaean overtones — as of a sin of the generations. Father Smulders, S.J., writes:

> When the Council of Trent teaches the transmission of original sin "by propagation, not by imitation," it indicates that man incurs original sin by entrance within fallen mankind. Procreation can include not only the strictly biological aspects, but also all the factors by which mankind makes someone its member, including education, environment, and example.[26]

Tresmontant has suggested that original sin is not so much the race inheriting the sin of an individual as the individual inheriting the sin of the race. Dubarle and Schoonenberg are more hesitant about identifying the accumulating sin of the world

---

[26] "Evolution and Original Sin," *Theology Digest* (Autumn, 1965), p. 175.

and original sin, though they think such an identification might
be made.

We shall discuss the sin of the world in the next section. Here
it is worth quoting Rahner on what, in his opinion, is the mini-
mum content of the Church's teaching on original sin:

> By "original sin" we must at least mean a general situation of
> damnation embracing all men prior to their own personal deci-
> sion, a situation which is nevertheless historic and not an essen-
> tial condition [that is, a condition belonging to their nature as
> such], one which has come to be through man and is not simply
> given in the fact of creatureliness.[27]

If belief in original sin and the gratuity of grace is retained
without our having recourse to an original couple who sinned
and handed on their sin by generation, it might be possible to re-
interpret the gifts said to have been given to Adam and Eve. We
have to ask: What is the message that the Church has for us
when she speaks of such gifts? The "moral-religious character
of the fall and original sin," writes Schoonenberg,[28] is uppermost.
Could it be that to speak of the loss of the gifts is a way of
teaching, accommodated to a bygone age though not necessarily
to ours, that man's helplessness in the face of evil is not simply
due to his creatureliness — for creatureliness as such, though
imperfect, is good — but to the disorder brought about by mankind's sin? As Dubarle writes:

> The doctrine of original sin consists in stating that not every-
> thing that worries us can be explained by the still incomplete
> development of man's spiritual powers or by the failures of the
> evolutive system that would leave room for mistakes or a process
> of trial and error on man's own level as well as on the level of
> the formation of the species. In the present state of humanity
> there is a disorder (not just something missing) on the religious
> as well as the human level, and this is the result of deliberate
> sin. Individuals are embroiled in this disorder whether they like
> it or not: and it is of small importance whether the point of
> departure was close to the animal state, as modern evolution
> theory thinks, or raised far above it, as was thought for a long
> time by theologians who did not have the information that we

---

[27] *Theological Investigations,* Vol. 1, p. 280.
[28] *Man and Sin,* p. 171.

possess today. The essential point is that the present state of mankind, with the baneful influence it exercises on newcomers to existence, is the result of deliberate faults and that even the initial religious state of young children is vitiated by it.[29]

We come back to a basic fact taught us by the Church, sometimes seemingly supported by unprovable, even false assumptions, and with the aid of a primitive world picture: men are not only sinners as individuals since they come into a world of sin and this world of sin is within them. From this disorder only God can deliver them; and he does so through Christ.

The sin of the world

Here we need to examine in more detail the collective state of guilt into which we enter at birth and which St. John calls "the sin of the world."

Probably in the consideration of sin both dogmatic and moral theology have concentrated too much on individuals. The former has focused too much upon Adam's sin and not enough upon all the sin that has accumulated from the time when man first appeared upon the scene. We need to take into account the sins of the Gentiles, the sins of the Jews, the rejection of God's messengers (the prophets and Christ), the iniquity of our own day. In moral theology the same tendency has been discernible: too often personal sins have been studied in isolation from the sinful state of society which is the condition, and often the proximate cause of the failings of individuals.

All this is, on the face of it, very surprising, for the doctrine of original (mankind's) sin should have sensitized us as nothing else to the community aspect of wrongdoing and godlessness. Mankind, as Genesis teaches, is one. It is one in good and evil, one in its hope and its destiny. This implies that it is not suf-

---

[29] *Op. cit.*, pp. 55–56.

ficient to look at man's nature abstractly or metaphysically, that is, outside the particularizing context of time-space. Man must be studied historically, for he is a historical animal and possesses a growing historical awareness. He must be studied socially, too, for he shares with his fellows a community — or society — situation.

Each individual is born at a particular moment into this community-situation. His freedom is affected by all the forces at work there. Freedom itself must not only be looked at metaphysically as if each of us has always (or nearly always) an absolute freedom of choice. We must, besides, examine freedom existentially. We have to ask: What choices are open to this individual here and now? The answer will always depend on innumerable factors, physiological, biological, social, historical, parental. We are not individuals who happen to be social but essentially social beings who gradually and imperfectly become aware of our individuality.

It is insufficient to say we are born into a situation of sin if this is taken to mean that we, being persons — individuals with intelligence and will — are able to stay untouched by such a situation. This we can never do. Being by essence social beings we are constituted by the very condition of society into which we are born. What if this situation is godless in the strictest sense? What if, by being born into this situation, we are powerless to reach God of ourselves? Then we are completely dependent on God to come and help.

Even when we are babies, of course, the influence of the world's sin is upon us. The child is most obviously a social creature. When he becomes self-aware his freedom is so situated that he begins to appropriate, to make his own, the condition of the world and to augment the sinfulness of it. As Hulsbosch puts it:

> Original sin is the powerlessness, arising from nature, of man in his incompleteness as creature to reach his freedom and to realize the desire to see God, *insofar* as this impotence is put into the context of a sinful world. . . .
> The history of prehistoric man inhabiting this earth thousands of centuries ago is a closed book to us; but in connection with

what has been said about the influence which the community asserts over the individual, it is possible to see mankind in its totality as the cause of the present state of affairs. Sin has taken root in the human community, in order to rule over it as a tyrannizing power. Whoever is born into this community is irrevocably delivered to this power.[30]

When the Baptist pointed out Jesus he said: "Behold the Lamb of God, who takes away the *sin* of the world" (Jn 1:29). There is a clear distinction in the scriptures between sins (*hamartēmata*) and sin (*hamartia*). The modern theologians are tending to agree with Gabriel Hebert's conclusion: "Here we have the distinction of actual sin and original sin. Actual sin is *acts* committed by such and such a person at such and such a time, by thought, word or deed; original sin is the *state* of alienation from God which lies behind."[31] The Christian gospel consists in the belief that escape from this enmity or alienation is provided by God himself and received by man as a gift.

We can summarize the above in this way. The truth which is depicted by the single couple (Adam and Eve) is the solidarity of mankind. The truth depicted by the fall is the solidarity of mankind in sin.

The sin of the world is not just the sum of personal (actual) sins committed by individuals. Man is an historical and social being. The sin of the world *as the world* is the sin of mankind as a community, not as a number of individuals. To take a parallel instance: the history of England is not what a number of private individuals have done as individuals over a number of centuries. There is a history of England which cannot be separated from the private life stories of individual Englishmen and yet which is not simply the sum of those private life stories. In short, the history of a nation is not the sum of the biographies of all the people who make up the nation. So the sin of the world is not the sum of the sins which human beings have committed.

Emphasis upon the sin of the world intensifies rather than weakens the notion of solidarity in sin. It encourages us to

---

[30] *Ibid.*, p. 56.
[31] *Op. cit.*, p. 26.

broaden the vision of the theological manuals.

Take the case of war. At the moment, only moral theology deals with this subject and then only to lay down the conditions for a just war. But, in the first place, dogmatic treatises should be interested in war as the expression and intensification of the sin of the world. (Perhaps we are witnessing here one of the many sad consequences of the often artificial separation of dogmatic and moral theology.) Not merely Adam's sin and the personal sins of individuals should be of interest to theology but also the state of mankind where armed conflict is often inevitable. What is there about man (and the human condition) that makes him wage war? It is too facile a solution to say it is all due to a legacy from an ancestor who lived and died millenia ago. The apologists who spoke of that alone were far too easily satisfied. Our misery is due to the sin of all mankind not to the misdemeanor of a highly gifted and despicable individual. Indeed, it might be argued that Christians have tended to blame Adam for all the ills and woes of the world and to exonerate the human race!

Moral theology should be concerned not only with laying down the conditions of a just war but in establishing a social situation in which war cannot occur. What would such a situation be like? How can such a situation be brought about?

A further instance. A race riot flares up in Los Angeles because colored folk object to a drunken Negro being arrested. The casual observer might say: "They are clearly in the wrong. They are seeking to obstruct the course of justice." That observer would be overlooking the fact that the arrest of the drunken Negro was only the spark that ignited the dry, waterless stubble of injustice which had been sedulously nurtured for generations. It is not that arrest alone, nor that arrest taken in conjunction with Adam's sin which caused the outbreak of black-versus-white fury. The cause was a *situation* of sin which had grown up over a period and which *neither* the white *nor* the colored folk of this generation are wholly responsible for.

Another example. Today man rightly prides himself on his

technological achievements. He sends rockets to the Moon, to Mars and Venus — while millions of the human race are dying of hunger and in despair. The fear of global war is considered to "justify" this unprecedented prodigality even at this historic moment when hunger — while it was never so widespread — can be abolished for the first time since the world began. Something is making us blind to brotherliness. It is the sin within us. It is making us refuse to build up a community in love. And yet this refusal is dominated not by our personal likes and dislikes but by a hate-situation into which all of us were born: the confrontation of the Marxist world and the Western alliance.

The Genesis story is a plea to us to realize that mankind is a community. It is one because of God, the creator, and his promise; and because of a network of sin whereby men are turned aside from God and attempt to thwart his promise. The New Testament clarifies and gives a new focus to this biblical doctrine when it presents Christ as the promised One of God. He it is who is to make men one. Sin is division because it is, at base, a rejection of him. In the light of this, sin, even before his coming, is seen to be a refusal to build up the community of love of which Jesus is the source and the heart.

Thus the final perspective of scripture is this: all sin is, in some respect or other, a refusal of Christ; a refusal to prepare for him, a refusal to accept him when he comes, a refusal to love him in his brethren.

Christ and creation

Classical theology has often seemed to suffer from a major defect: it has treated Christ as if he were God's second thought and not his first thought. Christ was considered exclusively (or almost so) as the restorer of a fallen world, as man's redeemer. The modern theologians, by contrast, are emphasizing the fact that Christ is, in addition, the intended fulfilment of creation. They seek to bring out Christ's cosmic rule, and for this the modern scientific world picture is indispensable.

Today science enables us to see that the whole of creation is a unity. This creation became human in man and then was humanized by him painfully and progressively. This ascending movement comes to its consummation in Christ for whom all things were made and in whom all subsist (Col 1:16).

On this thesis, creation and salvation must be integrated into a single divine idea or plan. Salvation is not something added to a world gone wrong but an aspect of creation coming to fulfilment. Christ came not simply to save but to fulfil; and the world he came to fulfil was not only an imperfect world coming to perfection but an imperfect world which had become sinful coming to perfection.

Karl Rahner tells us that though Christ's advent is, as it were, God's surprise, this "does not mean that we may not regard it in a perspective in which it appears as peak and conclusion, as the mysterious goal of God's plans and activity for his creation from all eternity."[32] The incarnation is not, according to this way of thinking, "something subsequent, a particular event *in* a world already *finished*," a kind of corrective on God's part when things went wrong. Christ's coming is the goal of everything. Everything leads up to him and prepares for him and assumes meaning because of him. "It is not pure fantasy," Rahner continues, "(though the attempt must be made with caution) to conceive of the 'evolution' of the world *towards Christ*, and to show how there is a gradual ascent which reaches a peak in him."[33]

What is at stake here is our grasp of the cosmic dimension of the incarnation.

> The Logos did not merely become (statically) man in Christ; he assumed a human history. But this is part of an entire history of the world and of humanity before and after it, and, what is more, the fulness of that history and its end. But if we take at

[32] *Theological Investigations*, Vol. 1, p. 164.
[33] *Ibid.*, p. 165.

all seriously the unity of this history, as centered upon Christ, it follows that Christ has always been involved in the whole of history as its prospective entelechy [that which gives a thing its form, purpose, direction].[34]

This is essentially the same as the vision of Teilhard de Chardin to whom most modern theologians acknowledge their profound debt even if they qualify their tribute in certain respects. Teilhard writes:

> The Kingdom of God is within us. When Christ appears in the clouds he will simply be manifesting a metamorphosis that has been slowly accomplished under his influence in the heart of the mass of mankind.[35]
>
> The world can no more have two summits than a circumference can have two centres. The star for which the world is waiting, without yet being able to give it a name, or rightly appreciate its true transcendence, or even recognize the most spiritual and divine of its rays, is, necessarily, Christ himself, in whom we hope. . . . We shall never know all that the incarnation still expects of the world's potentialities. We shall never put enough hope in the growing unity of mankind.[36]

It would seem that our youngsters need to be taught that Christ is not only the Savior but also the fulfiller of the world and all history. They are not satisfied when we say to them: "Christ came to save us from our sins." They sense that this is inadequate. "Why keep talking about sin?" they ask, and rightly. Christ also came to bring the beauty of the world to its consummation, to make men one and happy. This he is doing already though he will only finally accomplish his work when he comes in glory, to create a new heaven and a new earth.

Another reason, not as pragmatic as at first appears, why we must bring Christ's cosmic role into prominence today is this: unless we do, theology will be put out of business by science. Already science has, to a large extent, replaced theology: it is thought to be vastly superior to it intellectually and has even replaced faith as the harbinger of human happiness. This requires a word of explanation.

---

[34] *Ibid.*, p. 167.
[35] *The Divine Milieu* (New York: Harper & Row, 1964), p. 128.
[36] *Ibid.*, p. 154.

An unbeliever looking at the processes of the world and history might say: Man is an evolving animal, biologically but, even more so, socially. Centuries ago men were at war with one another, isolated and hateful. The world was in every way fragmented. This was inevitable. Races and nations didn't know each other; they didn't have the same culture or beliefs; they didn't speak the same language; they had few or no means of communication. The unification of the world has been made possible not by Christianity but by science, better, by man as a socially evolving animal. Christianity has been, by comparison with science, a minor unitive force in the world. Did the monasteries manage, with all their beneficence flowing from the love of Christ, to temper and sweeten the austere lives of the mediaeval poor? Who had the most lasting effect on the destitute, St. Francis of Assisi or the inventor of the steam engine? Will it be saints or nuclear scientists who will transform the lives of the under-privileged peoples of India, Africa, and South America?

The questions we have to ask ourselves must be of the same probing sort. What message has Christianity for the splendid, technologically advancing world in which our children are being brought up and of which they are justly proud? Is Christianity's only task to make scientists — those who "really unite the world" — more loving and Christ-like? Would not this be to fob off Christ with a rather trivial role? — as if the world goes on under its own powers and is influenced only indirectly by Christ when he shares his holiness with men. Isn't Christ more central to the progress of history than that? Isn't he the Man for whom the world was made, the one whom God had in mind when countless ages ago the cosmos first sprang into being? Doesn't the world progress to unification and perfection by reason of his influence?

Something along these lines must be developed in theology if, in our time, Christ is not to become of marginal interest even for Christians.

The ascending movement of which Christ is the secret origin is not without its crossings anrd obstructions. This is what sin consists in, as is clearly expressed in Genesis. Sin, like grace, has been in the world since the beginning. It is due entirely to man's contriving and issues in godlessness. This is why no one can reach God without God's help and intervention.

In the concrete, all men are to find communion with God in Christ. Father Rahner has argued that it is impossible to explain Christ's role as Savior of all men unless we hold monogenism. Monogenism alone, according to him, accounts for the unity of the race, so making it possible for one man to represent and die for all. The modern theologians, apart from finding this argument unclear, feel that it is unnecessary. Surely men are one because they are made by God, made for Christ, made to share a common destiny in Christ? It is not Adam and Eve who account for the unity of a race which Christ can then come and redeem. Father Rahner in stating that Christ is "the prospective entelechy" of the whole of history has given a better reason for the race's unity, namely, *Christ himself*. Christ's role is not only to restore, but to complete the world's making by reproducing his life of glory in men. He is able to restore *because* he has come to fulfil, and in the present order fulfilment *entails* restoration. He fulfils and saves in his body the Church which is, as it were, the space wherein men find freedom from the sin of the world "until he comes."

Since the Church is Christ's body, when we join the Church by baptism we may still belong *in* the world but we do not belong *to* it. Having escaped from the world's sin our situation has been radically transformed. We are transferred into Christ's kingdom. Here we are given power from on high to co-operate with God in building up the world.

We are free to accept God or reject him. We can choose sin, perdition, godlessness and death if we so wish. Since, as time goes on, man's self-consciousness and freedom as well as his technological powers grow, his choice for or against God, his option for faith or unbelief, are correspondingly intensified. He can choose to build up the universe or tear it down. This option has always been before him but never in such an obvious manner as now. Today it is possible for us to build up the world as an international community in love or to go in for massive, mutual annihilation.

In the New Testament we have noticed that sin is presented as basically a rejection of Christ. This rejection of him overturns the usual dimensions of history. It is not one fact among other historical facts, rather it conditions and affects all history. Christ is the only Righteous One, the only Bearer of God to the world, and the world's consummation. Mankind rejected him and so put itself completely outside grace. The crucifixion, according to some modern theologians, *is* the Fall of Man to which all the other falls contribute and on which they all converge.

For some, any refusal of God at the beginning of the race when sin first entered the world is not particularly noteworthy; for others, even if important, it is not to be compared with the rejection of Christ in the crucifixion. It is Christ through his redemptive suffering who shows us best what man is, how lost he is, how desperate his condition, how much he needs God to come and save. Could any sinner at the origin of mankind teach us all that God has taught us in the death of his Son? If we are not plunged in Christ's death but remain alienated from it we shall perish. It is by baptism that we are first plunged into that death and find salvation with the risen Christ.

The acceptance and the rejection of Christ goes on continually. This is the struggle between the "world" and Christ who has already overcome the world in principle. For Christ was raised from the dead on Easter Sunday. God has come and saved us. It is for men to appropriate that salvation which is in Christ's body the Church.

The promise of Genesis was that despite the sin of mankind God has pledged himself to come and save. Creation will come to its fulfilment despite the hindrance, the obstruction and darkness of sin. By reason of Christ's resurrection the Christian life is shot through with a burning optimism both on the personal level and on the level of world-community.

Conclusions

I have wanted, as far as possible, to stand apart from the controversies still raging and to describe them as objectively as I could; hence my own final comments will be very brief.

Certain things should be as evident to the reader as to me. First, the modern theologians are undoubtedly correct *in general* in their desire to read the scriptures and conciliar documents in their historical context. It is the historical perspective which is so often remarkably absent in the manuals, constructed as they are according to abstract schemes and compounded of metaphysical theses. Second, we have been given a far more vivid consciousness of the scope and depth of *mankind's* sin than we ever had before. This gain also is the result of an increased historical and social awareness. Third, the attempt — and it is an attempt which has scarcely begun — to bring out Christ's cosmic role is obviously needed in our time. It will certainly result in the recasting of some theological tracts and perhaps give a new sense of dynamism to all of them. Fourth, the modern theologians are desperately struggling to harmonize faith and science. It is only too easy, we know, for any purveyor of a new and possibly heterodox idea to point back to the "Galileo Incident" in order to make his opponents mitigate their accusations. The case, I believe, is rather different in the present instance. As Koestler remarked, of Galileo's condemnation: "The real danger of removing the earth from the center of the universe (was) . . . it undermined the whole structure of mediaeval cosmology."[37] It meant that much more hard thinking would have to be done in cosmology than most churchmen were prepared to do. What resulted from the condemnatory decree was not, as is often supposed, a slow-down of scientific research. It was Christianity, not science, that suffered. "What the decree conveyed to simple sons of the Church was that to talk of the earth's motion was a Bad Thing and contrary to faith; and what it conveyed to the skeptic was that the Church had

---

[37] Arthur Koestler, *op. cit.*, p. 465.

declared war on Science."[38] The modern theologians are cour-
ageously prepared to rethink the Church's teaching according to
the new scientific world picture which is far better authenticated
than Galileo's heliocentric opinion. (Galileo, after all, when he
so outraged the Holy See was only supported by an imperfect
telescope and an unproven theory and not by the prodigious
armory of today's scientific techniques, inventions, and observa-
tions.) They do not want the academic world to have fresh
grounds for thinking that churchmen are trying to make science
a branch of theology or that faith and reason are at war.[39]

Having said this I do not expect for a moment that all the
classical theologians are going to clamber out of their trenches
waving white flags of surrender. Why should they? Can it be
sensibly suggested that original sin is to be equated with "the sin
of the world" which so evidently affects people differently according to their age and environment? Surely, original sin is the
same in all of us? it will be asked. In what sense could baptism
be said to cleanse us, for good and all, of original sin if it be
conceived in this new way?

---

[38] *Ibid.*, p. 464.

[39] Father Thomas Corbishly, S.J., has written appreciatively of Teilhard de
Chardin's efforts in this field in his book, *The Contemporary Christian*
(Chapman, 1966). "The success of his approach to men who think instinc-
tively in evolutionary terms can hardly be overestimated. If today the scientific humanist is prepared to listen with anything approaching tolerance to
the utterance of Christian thinkers, this fact must be ascribed in no small
measure to the pioneer work of one who never concealed his deepest beliefs
yet could command respect as a scientist in his own right" (p. 84). "It is
no exaggeration to say that, in the sphere of the physical sciences in relation
to theology, no single man has done as much as Teilhard de Chardin to
prepare the way for a new presentation of the immutable truth entrusted
to the Church. Whereas for centuries the Church's teachers had gone on
repeating the language and imagery appropriate to an illiterate and un-
scientific tribe — the breath of God rippling the waters of a primeval chaos
and the like — the geologist, the biologist, the palaeontologist, and the
anthropologist have together developed a whole vocabulary and a world of
imagery to reveal the power working from within the very fabric of the universe to produce, on a time-space scale of unimaginable vastness, the gigantic
system contemplated by the eye of the microscope and the antenna of the
radio-telescope. It was the insight and the courage of Teilhard which not
only accepted this picture but saw it as the manifestation of that same
power of God at work in his world, more intimately and more surely than
anyone had ever realized" (p. 90).

It would seem to me, though I have not seen it stated in so many words, that the views of the modern theologians would lead to a different *approach*, at any rate, to the sacrament of baptism. As I understand it, infant baptism would, on their suppositions, remain the norm. By baptism the child would come into the Church where, throughout his development, he would have access to the abundant graces of the Spirit. But a child on the point of death would not be as desperately in need of baptism as one who is going to grow up beset by the sin of the world. (Baptism, on any score, must be looked at as a sacrament of the living rather than of the dying.) No one can enter heaven "with original sin on his soul" — but these modern theologians might claim that the babies by dying would die *out of* original sin which is no longer looked at in the simple fashion of "a stain" to be washed away. They have contributed nothing to the sin of the world. It has never come to life — "revived" to use Paul's word — in them. Limbo, as a theological hypothesis, would no longer be necessary, and certainly the present anxiety about baptizing foetuses would cease.

"Was there no 'original sin' at the beginning of the race?" the classical theologians would wish to ask. The reply would be, I suspect: "Of course, sin first entered the world at some moment or another but the precise moment is not important. The first sin (or sins) was not of decisive significance. That mankind as a whole is sinful, and that we are all embroiled in that sinfulness and rendered helpless by it — this is what really matters. The question, When exactly did sin first come into the world? admits of no exact answer, any more than does the question, When did you commit your first sin? All the evidence we shall ever have for answering the latter question is available and yet still we find it impossible to answer satisfactorily. It is not important anyway."

Classical theologians are likely to be impressed by much of what the modern theologians have written. Many of the advances made by the latter can be integrated into the classical presentation of original sin. They will most assuredly, however, balk at questioning, let alone denying, the existence of the protoparents of the human race. Both the nature of original sin and the implication of each member of the race in original sin become too nebulous without them. What was not clear to Pius XII in 1950, they will say, is still not clear to them. These theologians will, then, have to tackle thoroughly and honestly the not inconsiderable difficulties raised against their classical position. In addition, they will have to be reconciled, for the present anyway, to having the bulk of non-Catholic theology against them as well as the whole weight and prestige of modern science.

Index